# BACKROADS

*of the*

# CALIFORNIA
# WINE COUNTRY

# BACKROADS

### — of the —

## CALIFORNIA
## WINE COUNTRY

*Your Guide to the Wine Country's Most
Scenic Backroad Adventures*

TEXT BY KAREN MISURACA
PHOTOGRAPHY BY GARY CRABBE

Voyageur Press

## DEDICATION

To the wine lovers of the world, welcome to California!
And, to Michael, with whom I have shared the best times of my life
and so many unforgettable glasses of wine.—Karen Misuraca

To the memory of my dad, William, for his ever-present hand and guidance,
and to my sister, Leslie, and her family. "Cheers!" and a raised glass of
fine wine to you both, with lots of love.
—Gary Crabbe

---

First published in 2006 by Voyageur Press, an imprint of MBI Publishing Company, Galtier Plaza, Suite 200, 380 Jackson Street, St. Paul, MN 55101-3885 USA

Voyageur Press titles are also available at discounts in bulk quantity for industrial or sales-promotional use. For details write to Special Sales Manager at MBI Publishing Company, Galtier Plaza, Suite 200, 380 Jackson Street, St. Paul, MN 55101-3885 USA.

ISBN-13: 978-0-7603-2541-4
ISBN-10: 0-7603-2541-3

Editor: Josh Leventhal
Designer: Maria Friedrich

Printed in China

**ON THE FRONT COVER:**
*The sun sets over vineyards in the Carneros Region of Napa.*

**ON THE BACK COVER:**
*(top) Vineyards at Silver Oak Cellars, Sonoma County. (bottom left) Wagon and wine barrels at Jepson Vineyards, Mendocino County. (bottom right) Orr Springs Road near Ukiah, Mendocino County.*

**ON THE TITLE PAGE, MAIN IMAGE:**
*The rolling hills and lush vineyards of the Napa Valley at Calistoga, as seen from the Sterling Vineyards.*

**ON THE TITLE PAGE, INSET IMAGE:**
*Wine grapes ripening on the vine at the Parducci Wine Estates in Mendocino County.*

# CONTENTS

# INTRODUCTION

**FACING PAGE:**
*The moon rises over vineyards in Napa County's Carneros region.*

**ABOVE:**
*A sampling of Frey Vineyards wines, all produced from organic grapes grown in the Redwood Valley.*

A journey through California's wine valleys is a passage through the history of people and wine, beginning with Spanish padres who planted grapes for sacramental wines in the 1700s. The Gold Rush of the mid-1800s brought immigrants from around the world, particularly Italy, France, and Germany. The newcomers discovered verdant valleys, just inland of the coast, that had the look and climate of southern Europe's wine-producing regions. They settled here, planted their vineyards and food crops, and founded towns.

It was not until the 1970s, when premium California wines began to compete with the best of the French, that the wine country began to take on a certain mystique. The Napa Valley was for some decades considered to be "Wine Country," but recent years have seen several wine regions emerge. Each has a different human history and a unique combination of soil, terrain, and climate that determines the character of its wines. The actual growing environment is called the *terroir*, and the goal of the growers is to find the perfect *terroir* for each variety of grape, where the fruit can best manifest its flavor, color, and complexity.

Every wine has a soul, a temperament born of its birthplace. From the misty northern appellations of Mendocino County to the hot, dry flatlands of Paso Robles, in the wilds of the Santa Cruz Mountains and along the placid Russian River, each of the California wine regions has a spirit and a look of its own, captured in all its glory herein by Gary Crabbe's miraculous photographs.

We chose each of these driving tours for the singular sense of place created by remarkable scenery, historical significance, and a strong relationship to California-style winemaking. Caves and cellars, mansions and ranches, silent shady footpaths, and wildflower-strewn meadows are promised, along with a careful selection of wineries. Although some of the roads are narrow and remote, they are all easily navigable by a family sedan. You can complete each route in a day of leisurely driving and still have plenty of time for walks, picnicking, a taste of the grape, and other bucolic pleasures. Non-imbibers will be as entranced by the natural and historic attractions of the wine country as avid oenophiles will be with their new discoveries.

With the exception of the coastal areas, the California wine regions are warm and dry most of the year, so a sun hat or visor and several bottles of water are essential. Also on my list of "must haves" are walking shoes, so I can take short walks or hikes in the state and county parks; a camera and tripod; and binoculars to catch glimpses of peregrine falcons, red-tailed hawks, great blue herons, and bald eagles. In a basket, I keep a corkscrew, picnic gear, glasses (stemmed, of course), a sharp knife, a detailed map of winery locations, and a blanket. As I live in Sonoma, I am a wine collector; in my car I keep an empty cardboard wine carton, or an ice chest in summertime, in which to safely store bottles purchased at various wineries, wine-tasting festivals, and events.

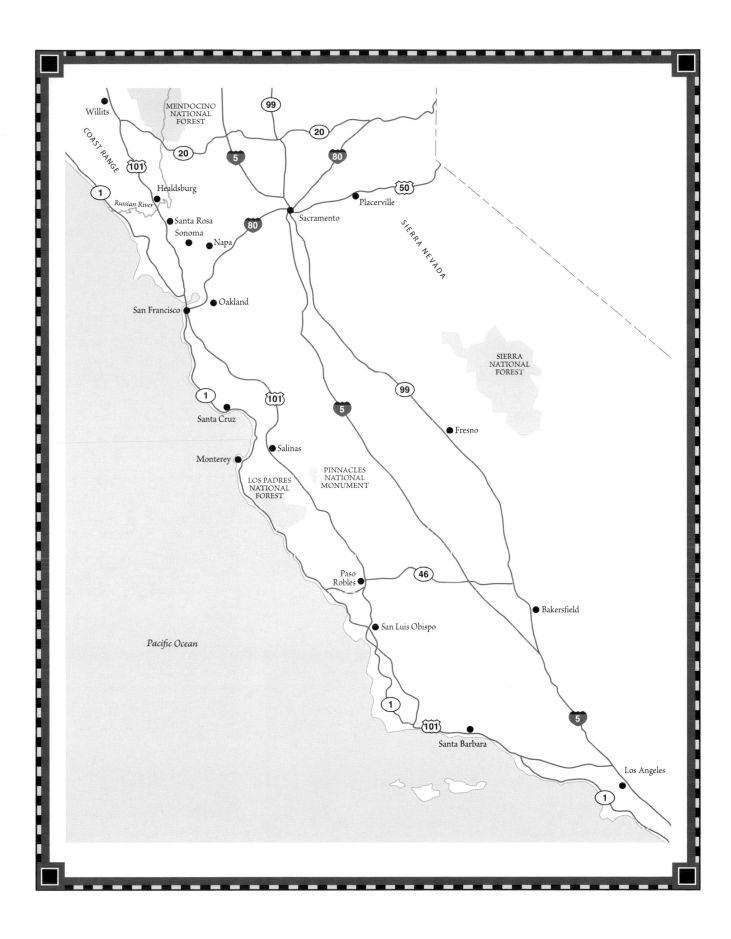

*Tasting rooms, such as this inviting spot at Jepson Vineyards near Ukiah, can be found throughout California's wine regions.*

*A country road meanders through the scenic countryside of Shenandoah Valley in Amador County, east of Sacramento.*

*A dramatic sunset over Napa Valley wine country.*

My favorite time of year to explore the California wine country is off-season: late winter through early spring. The vines are bare, the air is moist and fresh, and I am nearly alone at backroads wineries. I love to see the migrating birds in their striking colors and poses against the dramatic backdrop of trees and vineyards stripped of their foliage.

By mid-February or so, bright-yellow mustard and other cover crops erupt between the rows, and vineyard workers are seen carefully hand-pruning the vines down to a few fruiting canes and spurs. Budbreak occurs in April, when new green leaves unfold like Japanese fans and sleeping buds awaken. At their most fragile, the buds are protected from spring frost by whirling wind machines, smoke pots, and overhead water sprinklers.

June sees the flowering of tiny, delicate grape flowers, soon to develop into clusters. Vineyard workers again move through the rows, tying the fast-growing vines to trellises in order to support the heavy fruit to come.

Gaudy orange California poppies, red clover, and purple lupine are knee-high in midsummer, when the vines are full of leaves and ripening fruit. This is when I seek out far-flung wineries with the shadiest picnic sites, and I generally head north to where daytime temperatures are cooled by ocean breezes.

As the grapes ripen, some vineyards lighten the load of their canes by cutting away some of the bunches. Vines with lighter crop loads tend to produce intensely flavored grapes and more complex wine. Certain premium wineries remove as many as half of the clusters during "green drop."

The harvest begins in some appellations in August, and by September, the picking and the crush are on. Winemakers sample the ripening grapes, and the winery labs analyze the aroma, taste, sugar, and acidity, waiting for the exact day when the fruit is ready. When the signal is given, picking crews flood into the vineyards at the break of dawn, while the fruit is still cool. Using sharp, curved, hand-sized blades, they cut the bunches and drop them into tubs. When filled, the tubs are hoisted overhead and walked to gondolas—large open bins on wheels—between the rows. Tractors pull the gondolas to the waiting trucks, and the fruit is rushed to the crushing floors at the wineries. Within one or two hours of leaving the vines, the grapes are at the winery being de-stemmed in the crusher, then pressed and piped into holding and fermentation tanks. Cellar workers move quickly, receiving grapes from sunup to sundown.

Although you will not find yourself alone in the wine country during the crush, it is a heady time for a winery tour and for annual celebrations.

During the fall months, harvest festivals are held throughout the wine valleys. I often wonder how the winemakers find the time to take part in these events. Yet the winemakers and their crews, in T-shirts and cowboy hats splattered red, and boots muddy from the fields and wet from the slosh on the winery floor, turn out to celebrate each year's harvest with as much joy and anticipation as do we wide-eyed wine lovers who come for the food, the drink, and the merrymaking of the bacchanals.

Keep in mind that many of the premium wineries mentioned in this book are open by appointment only. With no exclusivity intended, these wineries have limited staff and may also have permit restrictions limiting the number of guest visits per day. When you call ahead, you will be warmly welcomed.

As you recline beneath the arms of an ancient oak tree on a warm afternoon, a crusty loaf, a chunk of cheese, and a glass of California wine at your elbow, gaze down the vineyard rows toward the distant mountains. This is the dream we promise you, that certain rapturous state of mind that comes when the sun and the wine warm your soul.

## VIVE LA DIFFERENCE!

Take a close look at the label on a bottle of premium California wine. When you see "Napa Valley" or "Chalk Hill," "Los Carneros" or "Guenoc Valley," you can be sure that at least 85 percent of the grapes were grown within a distinct region, legally termed an American Viticultural Area (AVA). These clearly delineated regions are also called appellations.

The French created the appellation system in the early 1900s to control the quality of their grapes. Vine diseases had decimated many of the French vineyards early in the twentieth century, and some wineries were importing grapes to sustain production, resulting in wines that were of inconsistent quality and no longer entirely French. In order to retain the character and integrity of what were then the world's best wines, the French instituted standards called *Appellation d'Origine Contrôlée* (AOC). In the late 1970s, the United States adopted its own system, loosely based on the French, to define AVAs.

Each AVA is entirely unique due to a combination of specific elements, including history, climate (there can be several microclimates within an AVA), soil type, elevation, and topography. Within the thirty-five-mile-long Napa Valley are more than a dozen AVAs—some on the gravelly, triangle-shaped "benches" formed by erosion at the foot of the mountains, some in the rich flatlands alongside the Napa River, some on steep, dry mountainsides. The Central Coast AVA encompasses a million acres of land, while the McDowell Valley AVA is just over five hundred acres.

Within the AVAs, it is the magical effect of *terroir* that creates the wine. To experience the mystery of *terroir* in one of the legendary Pinot Noirs from Santa Barbara County, hold your glass up to the light. Look at the luminous ruby color. Close your eyes and fill your nose with the aromas of black cherry, plum, oak, and clove, perhaps even coffee and walnuts. Feel the velvet

on your tongue, the warm spice in your throat. The vines that gave birth to the Pinot Noir grapes grew in foggy mornings and evenings and in hot, dry afternoons, their arms teased by the breath of the sea, their feet in stony, chalky soil.

As Galileo said, "Wine is light, held together by water."

*The Wine Advisory Board promoted California wines as a way to help you "live better." This 1954 ad proclaimed that wine can make food taste better, "for only a few cents a glass."*

# PART I

# THE NORTHERN COUNTIES:
# OVER HILLS AND DALES

*Cirrus clouds float above the hills of the Redwood Valley of Mendocino County.*

**ABOVE:**
*Mighty redwood trees tower at Montgomery Woods State Reserve in California's Coast Range.*

The wine valleys of Mendocino and Lake counties are some of the least visited and most rewarding in the wine country. Traffic and tourists are evident only on sunny weekends and then in low numbers. A sojourn to these inland wine regions is a leisurely ramble through sylvan valleys that recall a way of life long past, where time seems to stand still in a redwood forest or on a pine-fringed lakeshore.

The Mendocino wine region is in an area known as the Mendocino Plateau and is bounded by the Pacific Ocean, the mountains of the Coast Range, and the great northern redwood forests. Following the drainages of the Russian and Navarro rivers, tiny valleys shelter vineyards that rise from the river plains to rocky benchlands and up into the foothills. The most notable Mendocino wines are Zinfandels and Petite Syrahs from old vines, some planted a century or more ago, and rare varietals such as Barbera and Charbono.

Only fifty or so wineries are found in the ten viticultural areas of Mendocino County. In the cool-climate Anderson Valley, Pinot Noir and northern-European-style varietals, such as Riesling and Gewürztraminer, are prominent. The warmer, northern Russian River region around Hopland and the Redwood Valley is known for robust Zinfandels, Merlots, and Cabernets.

The up-and-coming winemaking region of Lake County has carved out four American Viticultural Areas (AVAs) so far. Fresh, grassy Sauvignon Blanc is a major varietal—just the wine to drink with your fresh catch from Clear Lake, the bass capital of the West.

*This illustration from* Harper's Weekly *in 1878 shows Chinese immigrant laborers working the winepresses at a California winery.* (Library of Congress)

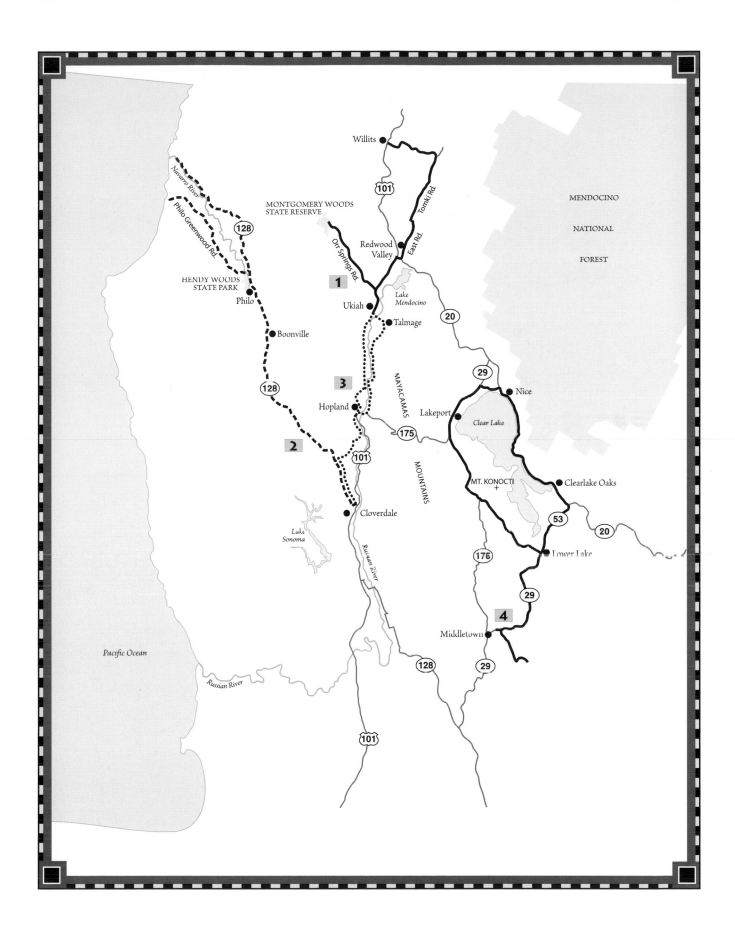

ROUTE 1

From Ukiah, head east on Vichy Springs Road; return to Ukiah and take U.S. Highway 101 north and Orr Springs Road west to the Montgomery Woods State Reserve. Return to U.S. 101, continue north, and take California Highway 20 east to Lake Mendocino and the Redwood Valley wineries off East Road. Follow East Road and Tomki Road north, then take Canyon Road west to Willits.

A driving tour through northern Mendocino County, between the Coast Range and the Mayacamas Mountains along the upper Russian River, is a quiet pleasure. The first non-native settlers arrived here in the mid-1850s to establish cattle-grazing pastures, fields of hops and grain crops, and fruit orchards. The building of the boomtown of San Francisco kicked off a thriving lumbering industry, too, which was sustained until the 1970s when redwood logging ended and winemaking began to support the economy. Today, Ukiah and Willits are humble communities that function as stopping-off points for wine-country explorers and travelers on their way to the Mendocino Coast.

The tremendous, primarily organic harvests of the small farms and orchards surrounding Ukiah are showcased at the town's twice-weekly farmers' markets. The markets feature vegetables, artisan cheeses, local honeys, and pears, for which the area is famous. Following the county's longtime trend of organically produced products is the Ukiah Brewing Company and Restaurant. At a Victorian-era bar moved here from San Francisco's Palace Hotel, patrons tap their toes to live music while they enjoy ales, lagers, stouts, and porters brewed with organic barley.

On South Main Street in a tree-shaded park, a 1911 California Craftsman–style home and a museum constitute the Grace Hudson Sun House, where Native American baskets and artifacts are on display. Exceptional here is a large collection of Grace Hudson's paintings of Pomo Indians, whom she painted at the end of the nineteenth century.

A small resort at Vichy Hot Springs, a California State Historic Landmark, lies on an old ranch east of Ukiah. Naturally carbonated, hot mineral waters bubble up from twenty thousand feet below into tubs and pools, as they did in the mid-nineteenth century when Mark Twain, Robert Louis Stevenson, and Jack London frequented the place. You can come for the baths, enjoy a massage, take a hike, or stay overnight in one of the nicely restored guest cottages, which are among the oldest structures in Mendocino County.

Orr Springs Road is a magical corridor through the Coast Range and some of the most pristine, undeveloped backwoods in the West. A former stagecoach route, the hilly road twists and turns between old homesteads and ranchlands that are still in the hands of families who settled here in the 1800s. Midway to the coast, a steep, winding road leads to Montgomery Woods State Reserve, where a walk beneath the arms of coastal redwoods can be an unforgettable experience. Walking trails trace Montgomery Creek upstream to five virgin groves that have never been logged. Among a magnificent stand of trees towering over 350 feet is the superstar, the Mendocino Tree; at 367.5 feet, it is the world's second-tallest living thing.

Just north of Ukiah, Parducci Wine Cellars has the look of an Italian

*PREVIOUS PAGES:*
*The early morning sky glows orange in the hills above Ukiah.*

villa, with vine-draped arbors, a clay-tile roof, and a splashing fountain. An immigrant from Tuscany, Adolph Parducci settled in the Ukiah Valley in 1912 and by 1932 had established the first winery in the county. Now the state's largest producer of Petite Syrah, Parducci is operated by the third and fourth generations of the family. Visitors sit under umbrellas on the cobblestone patio to taste the Syrahs and zesty, old-vine Zinfandels.

Every year, thousands of holidaymakers head for Lake Mendocino, a low-elevation, warm-water lake popular for water sports, camping, boating, and fishing for bass and catfish. On the north side of the lake, the Redwood Valley enjoys hot summer days and nights cooled by marine air flowing from the Pacific through a gap in the Coast Range; temperatures can dip as much as fifty degrees on a summer night. The combination of a long, dry growing season and volcanic "Redvine" sandstone soil, high in minerality and acidity, results in a *terroir* that produces low crop levels and intensely flavored, highly colored wines. Fewer than a dozen wineries, mostly family owned, are located on the red-dirt slopes of the Redwood Valley viticultural area.

Fife Vineyards, perched high above Lake Mendocino, is co-owned by Karen MacNeil, a prominent wine expert and author of *The Wine Bible*. Made from grapes grown on the rocky, fast-draining, south-facing slopes of the Ricetti Bench, MacNeil's jammy "Redhead Vineyard" Zinfandels express the distinctive Redwood Valley *terroir*, which is comparable to that of the Rhône Valley in France. The best-known Rhône-style wine from Fife is called L'Attitude 39. An unusual blend of Carignane, Syrah, Grenache, Mourvèdre, and Cinsault, the wine has a soft texture and spicy fruitiness. With its wide views of the lake and the countryside, the breezy picnic lawn at the winery makes a tranquil haven.

The barnlike winery building at Frey Vineyards lies in a dense wood in a luxuriant corner of the Redwood Valley on Tomki Road. John Frey was one of the originators of biodynamic and organic growing practices in Mendocino County. In addition to producing chemical-free grapes, he and his large family supply locals with organic vegetables and fruit. From vines planted by his father in the 1970s, Frey creates a creamy Chardonnay redolent of the toasted oak in which it ages, a plummy Syrah, and fruity Gewürztraminers. When you visit these scenic vineyards, notice what is planted between the rows—it may be garlic, brilliant red clover, herbs, or even watermelons.

The town of Willits, located in the middle of Mendocino County, was once the prosperous headquarters for nearly three dozen lumber mills. Originally hauling logs out of the redwood forests and to the mills in the 1880s, the Skunk Train—actually several historic diesel and steam trains—now takes passengers through the rugged terrain of the Coast Range and back along Pudding Creek, crossing thirty bridges and trestles. Near the train depot, a clutch of antique shops, bakeries, and bookstores is a reason to linger on the main street of Willits. The Mendocino County Museum here displays extraordinary Pomo basketry, railroad cars, and artifacts of early county history.

Orr Springs Road twists and turns through some of the
most pristine and dramatic landscapes in the wine country.

**CLOCKWISE FROM TOP:**
White deer can be seen roaming the woods of Ridgewood
Ranch near Willits. The deer were provided by William
Randolph Hearst in 1949.

Lake Mendocino is the perfect spot for some family fun on a
summer's afternoon.

Frey Vineyards, located in a rustic winery building in the
Redwood Valley, has been a pioneer in the production of
organically grown wine grapes.

The most famous name in Willits history is Seabiscuit, the notorious scalawag of a racehorse who electrified the American public with an unexpected series of wins during the Great Depression of the 1930s. After a stunning victory in 1938 over his rival—the larger, stronger Triple Crown winner, War Admiral—Seabiscuit and his jockey, the half-blind ex-prizefighter, Red Pollard, were both seriously injured. During the next year, the two of them slowly recovered on the hills and dales of Ridgewood Ranch, just south of Willits. In what was considered the comeback of the century by the horse of the century, Seabiscuit returned to Santa Anita in 1940 to win the Hundred Grander, the only prize that had eluded him.

Shortly thereafter, then the world's richest horse, the beloved Seabiscuit was retired to sprawling Ridgewood Ranch, and upon his death in 1947, he was buried under an oak tree at an undisclosed location there. The popular book and the movie, both entitled *Seabiscuit*, prompted new interest in the inspirational horse, and a limited series of guided tours is now made available to the public each year. With advance reservations, you can view vintage film footage, artifacts, and photos, and take a narrated walking tour of the barns and historic grounds at the ranch.

*Legendary racehorse Seabiscuit enjoyed the company of his canine friend, Pocatell, and his trainer, Tom Smith, in retirement at Ridgewood Ranch.*

## ANDERSON VALLEY
### ALONG THE NAVARRO

**ROUTE 2**

From Cloverdale, take California Highway 128 northwest through Boonville and Philo to the Pacific Coast. Alternatively, get on Philo Greenwood Road just north of Philo and proceed west to the coast at the town of Elk.

Rimmed by low mountains, the Anderson Valley is liberally watered by the Navarro River and three major creeks that serve as spawning grounds for salmon and steelhead trout. Through the narrow, sixteen-mile-long valley, California Highway 128 rambles through open meadows between a dark redwood and pine forest on the west and mixed hardwoods on the east. Mossy, split-rail fences and barns built in the nineteenth century are vestiges of the time when the valley was a remote logging and sheep-ranching area. The loggers are gone, yet sheep and cows continue to outnumber the three thousand or so residents.

In the 1970s, only two wineries operated in the Anderson Valley. Today, most of the twenty or so wineries are small and family operated, housed in rustic, often historic, farm buildings. You may find yourself on a personal tour with the proprietor, who is likely to be the winemaker, too. A few larger operations, including those making French-style sparkling wines, have elegant tasting rooms.

One of the first wineries at the south end of the valley, Maple Creek Winery, is accessed from Highway 128 by a short drive up a steep hill to the winery's rustic cabin. To announce your arrival, heed the "honk for wine" sign. Prepare to be greeted by the dogs, Lucy and Sheriff, and winemaker-owners, Linda Stutz and Tom Rodrigues. Chardonnays, Pinots, and more are produced here under the Artevino label.

Not much more than a short row of buildings along the highway, Boonville, the main valley town, is world famous for a bizarre American dialect called "Boontling," which was invented in the 1880s and is spoken only here. Around the turn of the nineteenth century, local farmers and shepherds made up the lingo as a way of avoiding strangers and having a few laughs. Today's visitors are puzzled by the Boontling signs advertising "Horn of Zeese" (cup of coffee) or "Bahl Gorms" (good food). The Buckhorn Saloon is a good place to sit a spell and listen to the strange speech. Be sure to have a mug of Boont Amber Ale or High Rollers Wheat Beer, brewed from water drawn from deep below the building. The microbrews are made at the Anderson Valley Brewing Company, where you can tour the three-story, Bavarian-style brew house.

Across the road from the saloon in an old roadhouse is the Booneville Hotel, which comprises a highly rated restaurant, a few simple, Shaker-inspired guest rooms, and a glorious overgrown flower and herb garden, where visitors laze away warm afternoons in hammocks.

In 1862, when the hotel was erected, more than three hundred thousand sheep grazed in Mendocino County. Although the wooly crop has long since passed its heyday, woolgrowers still gather every July for a lamb barbecue, sheep show, and sheep dog competitions at the Woolgrowers and Sheep Dog Trials. Another big annual event is the old-time Mendocino County Fair and Apple Show in September. Home-canned fruits, quilts, and 4-H livestock are on display; fresh apples, cider, pies, and local wines are on the menu. The fair's rodeo and a parade attract crowds.

Just up the road from town, Gowan's Oak Tree produce stand offers dozens of varieties of fruits and berries. It continues a tradition begun in 1880 by early settler George Studebaker, who filled his horse-drawn wagon with apples and peaches from his farm to sell to loggers and fishermen along the Mendocino coast. Today's owners, Cecil and Josephine Gowan, and their children open

*Navarro Vineyards of Anderson Valley has been specializing in German-style wines, such as Gewürztraminers and Rieslings, since 1974.*

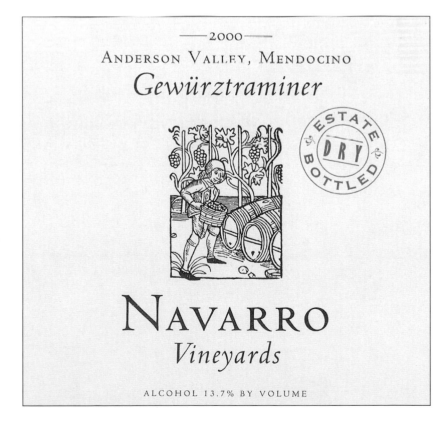

— 2000 —

ANDERSON VALLEY, MENDOCINO

*Gewürztraminer*

ESTATE DRY BOTTLED

NAVARRO
*Vineyards*

ALCOHOL 13.7% BY VOLUME

**RIGHT:**
*The Anderson Valley's sheep-ranching past is still evident as you explore the area's many wineries.*

**BELOW:**
*The family-owned Husch Vineyards has been producing fine reds on this charming estate since 1971.*

**ABOVE:**
*Pooches Lucy and Sheriff offer friendly greetings to visitors of Maple Creek Winery.*

**TOP:**
*The cool autumn weather brings color to the Maple Creek vineyards on the backroads of southern Mendocino County.*

**LEFT:**
*The paths of Hendy Woods State Park lead through spectacular stands of ancient redwoods.*

their orchards for wagon tours in April when the apple blossoms are fragrant clouds of pink and white.

Farther along Highway 128, Navarro Vineyards makes Alsace-style, dry Gewürztraminers and Rieslings, and some nonalcoholic "wines." In high demand, these wines are sold only in local restaurants and at the winery, where you can sit and sip under an arbor with a valley view. Next door Greenwood Ridge Vineyards, with its pond and backdrop of redwood groves, is a nice stop for a picnic.

French-owned sparkling-wine makers have arrived in force, right in the middle of the valley. Foggy mornings and nights and warm days create an ideal climate for Pinot Noir, a phenomenon that lured the company Champagne Louis Roederer, famous for Cristal, to establish Roederer Estate here. The estate's contemporary redwood winery is built into the hillside, and seekers of the bubbly step up to an antique zinc bar to taste citrusy L'Hermitage Brut, Anderson Valley Brut, and Brut Rosé. The glowing rose-colored terra cotta floor tiles came from a two-century-old chateau in France.

Once a chicken coop, the tasting room at Husch Vineyards Winery is now a rose-draped charmer. The oldest winery in the valley, Husch produces more than a dozen varieties of wine, including a notable flowery, fruity Gewürztraminer; the 1983 vintage was served at a state dinner in Beijing given by U.S. President Ronald Reagan.

Watch for the water tower and the white-balconied farmhouse at Handley Cellars. The Oaxacan, Balinese, and African art on display was collected by winemaker Milla Handley, the great-great-granddaughter of Henry Weinhard of brewing fame. Often the sparkling Sauvignon Blanc, the Chardonnay, the Pinot Noir, and the late-harvest wines from Handley are available only at the winery.

Heading north on Highway 128, cross the Navarro River and keep your eyes peeled for the sign to Hendy Woods State Park, which is off Philo Greenwood Road. Warmer and dryer than the Pacific Coast's rainforest-like redwood parks, this lesser-known preserve of ancient trees stands in magnificence on the banks of the Navarro. Two miles of forest trails lead to Big Hendy and Little Hendy groves, where thousand-year-old redwoods are nothing short of spectacular in size, reaching 270 feet. On the sandbanks and meadows along the river are picnic grounds and launching sites for kayakers and canoeists.

Departing the Anderson Valley on the way to the Mendocino Coast, Highway 128 tunnels through ferny glens and dense groves of second-growth redwoods that hug the road and filter the light into flickering shafts.

# HOPLAND AND THE McDOWELL VALLEY
## VINEYARDS AND FARM TOWNS

In the inland valleys on the southern end of Mendocino County, temperatures rise into the hundreds in the summertime and sink below zero on some winter nights. The climate is ideal for growing Bartlett and Anjou pears, as well as wine grapes.

Wrapped snugly with vineyards and farmlands and hardly a mile long, Hopland is a one-horse town with a sophisticated undertone. Art galleries, antique shops, winery tasting rooms, small cafés, an imposing old hotel, and a laid-back beer hall make up the attractions.

Like a well-preserved dowager in splendid Victorian dress, the impressive Hopland Inn features peaked dormers and sweeping verandas. Dark and comforting, the bar is distinguished by a remarkable collection of single malt scotch whiskeys. With glasses of the silky golden stuff at hand, guests are often seen in the library, where floor-to-ceiling shelves are lined with books, and wingback chairs and sofas are pulled up to a roaring fire in the green-marble fireplace.

People who favor the taste of the hop are found across the street at the Mendocino Brewing Company, in a brick building that in the 1880s was the Hop Vine Saloon. At the fancy bar beneath the original stamped-tin ceiling, you can try Red Tale and Blue Heron ales, Black Hawk Stout, and White Hawk IPA, among other full-bodied brews. When the aroma of baking bread wafts across your nose, step next door for some of the rustic artisan breads that emerge from the wood-burning stone ovens at Phoenix Bread Company. Try the three-pound Scottish harvest bread called Struan, or the savory loaf stuffed with Kalamata olives, oregano, and sun-dried tomatoes.

Shops in Hopland offer handcrafted treasures, such as casual furniture made of willow harvested from the banks of the Russian River, and sweaters and throws knitted from the wool of local sheep. More than five thousand heritage roses bloom in a plaza, and several well-used bocce ball courts are reminders of Mendocino's historic contingent of Italian winemakers, who are well represented by tasting rooms right in the middle of town.

Owned by the venerable Parducci family, who have made wine here since before Prohibition, McNab Ridge Winery is the oldest winery in the county. Their vineyard property was originally homesteaded in 1868 by Alexander McNab, a Scottish immigrant famous for introducing the McNab sheep dog to the United States.

A few steps away from McNab Ridge Winerey is the tiny Graziano Family of Wines tasting room, where you can choose from more than two dozen mostly Italianate wines, from Nebbiolo, Tanaro, and Peppolino to the rare Pinot Meunier. Winemaker Gregory Graziano is the grandson of Vincenzo, who is rumored to have supported his family during Prohibition by shipping his wines to speakeasies in the eastern states.

## ROUTE 3

Beginning in Hopland, take California Highway 175 east to Fetzer Vineyards. Go north on Eastside Road to Talmage, and south on U.S. Highway 101. Take County Road 112A west, then return to U.S. 101 and continue south to Hopland. Drive south on Mountain House Road and east on California Highway 128 to Cloverdale.

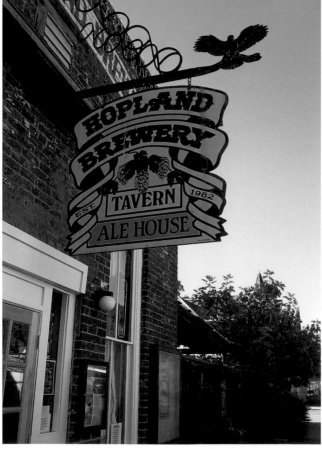

**ABOVE:**
*This lovely tree-lined drive leads to Fetzer Vineyards, a wholly organic winery and the sixth-largest premium wine producer in the country.*

**LEFT:**
*Mendocino County has more to offer than just fine wines. The Mendocino Brewing Company has been serving its finely crafted brews at the Hopland Brewery since 1983.*

**FACING PAGE:**
*The warm valleys around Hopland offer an ideal climate for growing grapes as well as apples and pears.*

Just east of Hopland, the McDowell Valley is more of a high sloping bench than a valley. At about a thousand feet in elevation, it drains towards the nearby Russian River. Planted in the early twentieth century, Syrah and Grenache vines continue to thrive. McDowell Valley Vineyards owns most of the vineyards in this AVA and specializes in Rhône-style wines such as Viognier, Marsanne, Syrah, and Grenache Rosé. Owner and winemaker Bill Crawford is dedicated to the propagation of the Rhônes and has gathered what may be the state's largest collection of Syrah clones. His Syrahs are big, age-worthy, spicy wines with jammy, berry flavors, while the summery Grenache Rosé is a dry, floral, and fruity concoction. McDowell's Western-style tasting room in Hopland is loaded with whimsical décor, including a twelve-point elk head and a fascinating display of Alaskan and Canadian Inuit masks.

When wine perks up your taste buds, step next door into the Bluebird Cafe, where the menu lists burgers made of beef, buffalo, elk, ostrich, wild boar, and kangaroo. Save room for homemade berry pie.

An elm-lined lane out of town leads to Fetzer Vineyards Valley Oaks, a multifaceted destination for wine and food enthusiasts. The country's largest producer of organically grown grapes, Fetzer is a winery with a mission. In 1984, it pioneered efforts to establish sustainability in its vineyards by eliminating chemical pesticides, herbicides, fungicides, and fertilizers. Its efforts began with a Zinfandel vineyard that was originally planted in the 1860s in what is now the Mendocino Ridge viticultural area. Today, Fetzer's Bonterra wines, made from the chemical-free grapes, are certified 100 percent organic. In addition, the winery's energy-conservation efforts won recognition from the White House in 1994.

On Eastside Road in the village of Talmage, drive through a massive, pagoda-like golden gate to enter the City of Ten Thousand Buddhas (CTTB), a retreat center where robed Buddhist monks, scholars, and a flock of peacocks welcome visitors. In the Jeweled Hall of Ten Thousand Buddhas, small, gilded Buddhas—in fact, ten thousand of them—gleam in niches around an eighteen-foot-tall figure of Guanshiyin Bodhisattva.

At Jeriko Estate, on County Road 112A a mile north of Hopland, a mirage of Mediterranean architecture seems to float against the forested hillsides on the banks of the Russian River. Organically cultivated grapes are grown for a unique, citrusy, sparkling Chardonnay and for Italian and Rhône varietals. Spend some time here enjoying the art collection, walking trails, and picnic grounds.

From Hopland, a springtime driving trip on the winding Mountain House Road is rewarded with carpets of purple hyacinths, pink columbine, and buttercups. California poppies and yellow and purple lupine take over in the summer. This route was once part of the stagecoach road that ran from Ukiah to San Francisco. As you descend toward California Highway 128, vineyards at the edge of the Yorkville viticultural area come into view.

# LAKE COUNTY
## SHORELINE LOOK, SMALL-TOWN CHARM

An extinct volcano topping out at 4,200 feet, Mount Konocti dominates the rolling countryside of Lake County, which is as green as Ireland in spring and winter, and dry and golden in summer and fall. The mild winters are a good time for fishing expeditions, hunting for agates and opals, and bird watching. On a hike or a boat ride, you will see great numbers of waterfowl and migrating birds from Alaska and Canada, and you may see over wintering bald eagles, too. The county has the greatest variety of bird species in the state.

When school's out, families arrive at Clear Lake en masse with their boats, camping gear, and water sports equipment. The lake is ringed with casual vacation resorts, marinas, and campgrounds. Quiet country roads winding through orchard lands and volcanic hills are designated as the "Lake County Pathways" for biking and walking.

One of the first winery founders in Lake County was the Victorian-era stage actress and social powerhouse, Lillie Langtry, the most famous—or infamous—woman in Great Britain at the time. Langtry purchased several thousand acres in an idyllic corner of the Guenoc Valley, planted vineyards, and imported her own winemaker from Bordeaux, France. A painting of the lovely, young "Jersey Lily" appears today on the bottle labels of Guenoc and Langtry Estate Vineyards and Winery. The winery is located on her original estate in a rare single-winery appellation, the Guenoc Valley viticultural area. A vine-covered arbor leads to a tasting room filled with vintage portraits and memorabilia of the estate and the region.

On the north shore of Clear Lake, between Lucerne and Nice, a tile-roofed, thick-walled Spanish-style hacienda houses the Ceago Del Lago winery, whose biodynamically farmed vineyards produce Cabernet, Merlot, and Sauvignon Blanc grapes for award-winning wines. Visitors stroll in the extensive gardens, along a mile of undeveloped shoreline, and onto the 340-foot pier on Tule Bay, the longest pier on the lake.

Just north around the lake, thirty thousand tulip bulbs burst into bloom in time for the Tulip Festival in March at Tulip Hill Winery and Vineyards on Bartlett Springs Road. The winery's grape-growing efforts have paid off in their Mount Oso Reserve Cabernets and Chardonnays and in the Merlot/Syrah blend "White Mirage," a spicy, summery concoction aromatic of strawberry, rhubarb, and rose petals.

Pressing on around the lake's north shore, consider a stop at the county seat, Lakeport, where a lineup of historic buildings on Main Street, an old-fashioned band shell, and a grassy lakefront park are the main attractions. The 1871 Lake County Historical Courthouse Museum displays hundreds of Pomo, Wintun, Wappo, and Lake Miwok Indian baskets—examples of what experts believe are some of the finest decorated baskets ever created by indigenous peoples.

## ROUTE 4

From Middletown on California Highway 29, take Butts Canyon Road southeast to Guenoc Winery. Return to Highway 29 and proceed north. Take California Highway 53 north and California Highway 20 west around Clear Lake and through Clearlake Oaks and Nice. Take the Nice-Lucerne Cutoff Road west to Highway 29 south to complete the lakeshore loop and return to Middletown.

*Mount Konocti, illuminated by the setting sun, looms large above this Lake County vineyard.*

**TOP:**
*Peaceful at sunrise, Clear Lake State Park is a popular recreation spot in the up-and-coming wine region of Lake County.*

**ABOVE:**
*The Ceago Del Lago winery brings a distinctly Mediterranean flavor to Lake County, as well as an innovative approach to biodynamic farming.*

**LEFT:**
*The vibrant flower gardens of Tulip Hill Winery include more than just tulips.*

Although biodynamic farming may sound high-tech, it is based on traditional, Old World techniques using natural, sustainable resources to nurture and protect grapevines. Turning away from chemically synthesized fertilizers, pesticides, and herbicides, many California wineries are feeding their vines with compost prepared from manure, straw, and other vegetative matter collected on-site. Rotated cover crops and mechanical methods control weeds and conserve water.

At Ceago Del Lago in Lake County, a flock of about forty Rambouillet sheep keep grasses and weeds nipped down. Rhode Island Red chickens roam the vineyards, foraging for cutworms that might otherwise damage vine roots—and they provide eggs for the ranch staff.

Into compost piles go branches of estate-grown herbs, chamomile, dandelions, oak bark, and ground-up cow horns, which enhance the growth of microorganisms. The rich compost mixture is applied during the most auspicious days of the lunar cycle. Even the tules that grow along the Clear Lake shoreline are used as grapevine ties.

Founded out of concern for consumer health and the environment, the fast-growing biodynamic movement among grape growers and other farmers in Lake County is the ultimate expression of *terroir*, the concept of the taste and quality of wine being an expression of where and how the grapes are grown.

*The portrait of British actress Lillie Langtry adorns the wine labels for the winery she founded in the Guenoc Valley more than 150 years ago.*

Located in a walnut orchard between Lakeport and Kelseyville, Steele Winery welcomes visitors to lake-view picnic grounds under the trees. Jed Steele was a pioneer in the world of California winemaking, particularly in the development of Chardonnay. Before establishing his own winery here, he spent five decades blending millions of gallons of wine for some of the top wineries in the state—notably Edmeades, Stony Hill, and Kendall Jackson. Lovers of Chardonnay, Pinot Noir, and Zinfandel congregate at the winery in October for the annual Harvest Festival, a bacchanal of grape stomping, music, food, and, of course, wine.

As you continue on California Highway 29, slow down for Ployez Winery, south of Lower Lake. Winemaker and owner Gerald Ployez grew up in the Champagne region of France, where three generations of his family produced bubbly. He employs the traditional *méthode champenoise* to make his Ployez NV California Brut sparkling Chardonnay. Other Ployez varieties include a bright, cherry–smoky-raspberry Gamay Beaujolais and a Cabernet suggestive of red currant and plum. Both wines are consumed with jubilation at the annual Clear Lake Jazz Festival in June, on the grounds of the redwood-sided winery.

# PART II

# SONOMA COUNTY:
# COUNTRY LANES AND RIVER VALLEYS

**FACING PAGE:**
*A distant moon sets beyond a winter vineyard in the Valley of the Moon.*

**ABOVE:**
*The European-inspired courtyard at Chateau St. Jean in Kenwood features a statue of the winery's namesake.*

**LEFT:**
Vineyards stretch across the Alexander Valley in northern Sonoma County.

**TOP RIGHT:**
A roadside signpost points the way to many of the Alexander Valley's thirty-plus wineries.

**BOTTOM RIGHT:**
Red-wine grapes and autumn leaves in the Alexander Valley.

the growing season and resulting in high acidity and fruit-forward flavors.

Driving on Souverain Road, it is hard to miss the sight of the steep blue-slate roofs of Chateau Souverain, an architectural cross between a French chateau and a Sonoma County hop kiln. Sipping a chocolatey Merlot on the terrace of the restaurant while gazing out into the sweeping vineyards and the Mayacamas Mountains beyond can be a lyrical experience. A stone and redwood winery building up Geyserville Avenue, Canyon Road Winery offers old-vine Zinfandels and other varietals, and you can linger to picnic and play bocce ball.

In October when the sky is sparkling clear and vineyards are aflame in reds and golds, their fruit safely harvested, the residents of the Alexander Valley gather for old-time fun at the Fall Colors Festival in Geyserville. With a trove of carefully preserved vintage buildings, Geyserville is as quaint as a wine-country town can be. In the century-old Geyserville Bank Building, Meeker Vineyard offers pours from hand-painted bottles of Bordeaux blends with whimsical names, such as Four Kings, the Winemakers' Handprint Merlot, and the Halloween blend, Blankenheim's Frankenstein.

A former stagecoach stop is now the Geyser Smokehouse, where wooden floors, a stamped-tin ceiling, a rusted hay baler, and an antler chandelier create a cowboy roadhouse setting. Locals and Harley riders belly up to the bar for microbeers, while Texas-style ribs and burgers are cooked over an aromatic smoker that is fed by oak, apple wood, and Chardonnay vines. Bosworth and Son General Merchandise, a buggy shop in 1902, is a sort of museum and an emporium of Western gear. Harry Bosworth and his black lab, Buster, will sell you a pair of red cowboy boots, a ten-gallon hat, a Western saddle, livestock feed, or a souvenir bandana.

Between winery visits, travelers rest overnight at two glorious old inns that face each other on the main street of Geyserville: the Eastlake- and Stick-style Hope-Merrill House, her gingerbread trim as pretty as it was in 1885, and the Hope-Bosworth House, a 1904 Queen Anne Craftsman framed by tall palms.

On California Highway 128 at Alexander Valley Road is the Jimtown Store, a general store like no other. The green and yellow, circa-1860 building is jam-packed with old-fashioned toys and penny candies, local organic produce and wines, antiques and folk art. You can pick up a boxed lunch here at the deli or have a picnic on the patio.

Twenty or so wineries are scattered in the Alexander Valley viticultural area along Highway 128 and on a few country roads that connect with the Dry Creek and Knights valleys. This is prime Cabernet country. To buy Johnson's Alexander Valley Cabernet Sauvignon, you must stop in at the small winery, accessed by a short, often rough, road. Expect to be greeted by an old tractor and two basset hounds. When you buy a bottle, a one-thousand-pipe organ plays the theme from *Phantom of the Opera*.

A fine vantage point for valley views is the oak-shaded picnic grounds at Field Stone Winery, where the crisp, lemony Viogniers, and other varieties, stay chilled in massive stone cellars.

A bucolic corner of northern California and a handful of premium wineries in their own tiny AVA are waiting to be discovered on eight miles of narrow, two-lane Chalk Hill Road, which winds through open grazing meadows and oak-studded fields in the foothills of the western Mayacamas Mountains. A subappellation of the Russian River Valley viticultural area, Chalk Hill is characterized by shallow, rocky, whitish soil, derived from ancient volcanic eruptions from nearby Mount St. Helena. Fruit-concentrated, highly flavorful wines result from the combination of poor soil, warm summers, and cool nights.

Lancaster Estate offers a guided tour that includes a drive through the vineyards, a stop at the winery, a look inside the gigantic aging caves, and glasses of luscious Bordeaux-style Cabernets.

A grand entrance through an olive grove leads to lakes, gardens, and a villa at Chateau Felice where you can try gold-medal-winning Syrahs and Cabernets. An Englishman and former aeronautical engineer, Barry Rodgers, and his wife, Phyllis, are the proprietors, and their daughter is the winemaker of the twenty-five-acre estate winery.

With the harvest from sixty different vineyards, Chalk Hill Estates Vineyards and Winery makes estate-bottled wines such as bright, spicy Chardonnays with flavors of pears and pineapple. English gardens and a stunning backcountry setting make this estate one of the prettiest staging areas for a winery tour and tasting experience.

## THE FIRST PIONEER

An adventurous Pennsylvanian who had tried his hand at fur trapping in the Rockies and gold mining in California, thirty-five-year-old Cyrus Alexander rode horseback from San Diego to the Alexander Valley in 1840. He had been hired by Captain Henry Fitch to find several thousand acres suitable for ranching. Acquiring the land from the Mexican government, Fitch asked Alexander to establish and run the ranch. There he was to manage the care and breeding of a thousand horses, plus huge herds of cattle and sheep. The reward for his labors was a large parcel of land on the eastern side of the Russian River, where he built a home for his large family on a knoll alongside a creek. That house is now the home of the Wetzel family, owners of Alexander Valley Vineyards. Among their award-winning wines, the "Cyrus" Cabernet blend is a spicy, oaky concoction, intensely redolent of black cherry and cassis—a fitting tribute to the audacious pioneer.

Cyrus Alexander built the valley's first schoolhouse, which is now a charming guesthouse for the Wetzels.

*Pioneer Cyrus Alexander established a sprawling* rancho *in the valley that later bore his name, in the heart of Sonoma wine country.*

Under a huge oak tree behind the winery, Cyrus and Rufina Alexander are buried, along with five of their ten children. In Healdsburg, a vividly ornamented bed-and-breakfast inn, the George Alexander House, is the Queen Anne Victorian built in 1905 by Cyrus' tenth child, George, and his wife, Nellie.

**FACING PAGE:**
*Downtown Geyserville is lined with charming buildings dating from the town's nineteenth-century origins.*

**ABOVE:**
*The tasting room at the Field Stone Winery is housed in the winery's stone cellars.*

**LEFT:**
*The Alexander Valley comes alive with reds and yellows in autumn.*

# DRY CREEK VALLEY
## OLD-TIME TOWN, OLD VINE ZINS

### ROUTE 6

From Healdsburg, take Mill Street west to West Dry Creek Road and turn north. Follow West Dry Creek Road to Wine Creek Road, which runs west to Michel-Schlumberger wine estate. Return to West Dry Creek Road and continue north to a mile past the Yoakim Bridge. Return to the bridge and go east over the bridge to Dry Creek Road, turning north to Lake Sonoma. Return south to Healdsburg on Dry Creek Road.

Where the Alexander, Russian River, and Dry Creek valleys meet, the picture-perfect town of Healdsburg was established in the mid-1800s by Harmon Heald, an Ohioan who had traveled west by wagon train in search of gold. He built the first home in the area and sold goods to local Native Americans and settlers. In 1867, he purchased a large tract of land, laid out lots in a network around a Spanish-style plaza, and sold them for fifteen dollars each. Today, covered by a canopy of tall redwoods, palms, and magnolias, the plaza is still the heart of the town. Visitors take slow strolls around the block-square greensward, enjoying the shops and cafés.

Driving out of Healdsburg over the Mill Street bridge, you get your first glimpse of Dry Creek, a burbling stream overhung by cottonwoods and silvery willows. At the Mill Street–West Dry Creek junction is the archway entrance to Madrona Manor, one of California's largest and most elaborate Victorian-era architectural masterpieces, complete with lacy gingerbread and scrollwork trimmings, a mansard roof, columned verandas, and a spectacle of dormers. A huge, Greek Revival mansion built in 1881, it is now an inn and restaurant, and you are welcome to stop by for a tour of the glorious gardens and grounds.

On twisting, turning West Dry Creek Road, mossy oak branches touch overhead, split-rail fences line the vineyards, and worn-looking farm buildings turn up around the bends. Behind a filigreed gate, a Mediterranean-style hacienda with a tile roof and a bell tower marks the Michel-Schlumberger wine estate. The proprietor, Jacques Pierre Schlumberger, descends from a family famous for winemaking in Alsace, France, for more than four hundred years. Sprawling across rocky benchlands in the canyon are rows of his Bordeaux-type grapevines. The estate produces a mere fifteen thousand cases a year, including an elegant Cabernet Sauvignon tasting of blueberry, cassis, and hints of earthy cedar aromas.

Farther up West Dry Creek Road, where it tapers to one lane just north of the Yoakim Bridge, proceed at a snail's pace a half mile or so to where dark vines grow right up to both sides of the road. Winter, when the vines are bare, is the best season to really get a look at these old geezers. Rooted in the volcanic soil, they look like grizzled, ancient gnomes, their fingers flailing from stubby, twisted, muscular arms. Growing on gravelly benchlands and hillsides, and on the valley floor in reddish, clay loam, the old vines are the riches of the valley. To be designated as "old vine" they must be at least fifty years old. When you explore the California wine country, you will notice that these thick, low-to-the-ground vines no longer exist in most of the state's vast winelands, a fact that contributes to the romantic sense of place here. Dry Creek Valley has the densest concentration of old-vine Zinfandel vineyards in the world. The grapes produce spicy, full-bodied reds, redolent of blackberry, black cherry, and black currant and often having peppery overtones.

Tucked away on this upper end of West Dry Creek Road, Lou Preston of Preston Vineyards has been farming organic, chemical-free grapes for over thirty years. An acclaimed baker, Preston bakes bread in his *forno*, a wood-fired oven. Visitors to the tasting room can purchase his delicious breads or take away some homegrown olives and olive oil. On Sundays, bring your own jugs to fill up with "Guadagni Red," a blend of Italian varietals—Zinfandel, Malvoise, and Carignane—available only at the winery and only on Sundays.

A pleasant place to stop for a rest or a picnic on Dry Creek Road is Ferrari-Carano Winery. In contrast to the backwoodsy appearance of most of the Dry Creek wineries, Ferrari-Carano was built to impress. Fancy iron gates open to a grand vista of lush gardens and an Italianate mansion adorned with stone columns, vine-draped arches, and Roman-tile roofs. Wine lover or not, you will enjoy seeing the public tasting room, all polished mahogany, mirrors, and black granite; and don't fail to tiptoe down the stone stairs into the magnificent vaulted cellar where red wines age in over a thousand French oak barrels. Above the valley on the mountainsides, shallow, rocky soils and low yields produce grapes of intense flavor for the winery's unique Tresor blend of the five classic Bordeaux varieties: Cabernet Sauvignon, Merlot, Malbec, Cabernet Franc, and Petit Verdot.

At the north end of the valley, Lake Sonoma lies deep in a wilderness of craggy mountains, which are often wreathed in wispy clouds or fog from the ocean. Bass fishing is good here most of the year, and camping sites are many. Hikers often catch sight of the rare peregrine falcons that nest in the area. The hawklike birds have slate-gray backs, white bibs, white and gray barred bodies and legs, and black sideburns. Nearly extinct in the early 1970s, their populations are now in recovery.

Returning south towards Healdsburg, you will see wide views of vineyards blanketing the valley floor. Earlier in the century, Dry Creek farmers grew primarily plums, apples, and peaches. Vines had gradually replaced nearly every fruit tree by the 1980s. Nonetheless, the Waltenspiels at Timber Crest Farms continue, as they have for nearly five decades, to produce organic fresh and dried fruits, including their specialty, sun-dried tomatoes. Also on Dry Creek Road, the Family Wineries Tasting Room offers samples of estate-bottled varietals from six small premium wineries.

One more place to buy wine, pick up a fishing license, or order a deli sandwich is the delightfully old-fashioned Dry Creek General Store, where denizens of the valley are often found at the bar. Cold beer seems to be the drink of choice here.

**TOP:**
*The rugged Pritchett Peaks rise high above Lake Sonoma.*

**RIGHT:**
*Lake Sonoma was created in 1983 with construction of the Warm Springs Dam. Today it is a popular destination for fishing, boating, hiking, and other outdoor activities.*

**FACING PAGE, TOP:**
*The Dry Creek General Store harks back to an earlier time—other than the line of motorcycles parked outside.*

**FACING PAGE, BOTTOM:**
*Oak barrels contain the alluring wines of Lambert Bridge Winery in the heart of the Dry Creek Valley.*

## ROUTE 7

From the junction of U.S. Highway 101 and Westside Road in Healdsburg, drive south on Westside Road to River Road. Follow River Road west to Guerneville. Head north on Armstrong Woods Road to explore the Armstrong Redwoods State Reserve, then return to Guerneville and take California Highway 116 west to Duncans Mills.

Flowing out of mountains north of Ukiah, the Russian River winds through redwood canyons, past sandy beaches, alongside orchards and vineyards, and slides calmly all the way to the sea at Bridgehaven. In winter, ocean waves clash with the river in a stormy drama, while seals hide in the river's mouth to give birth away from the sharp eyes of hungry sharks and whales.

In the mid-1800s, tourists from San Francisco rode ferries across the bay and hopped onto a narrow-gauge railroad that stopped at a string of resorts along the Russian River. When the motorcar arrived on the scene, city dwellers were lured farther afield; lumbering declined around the same time, and river towns fell into a deep sleep. The little burg of Guerneville managed to thrive through the Big Band era when Benny Goodman and Harry James kept the revelers coming. That heyday faded until the 1970s when the tremendous growth of wineries began a new era of tourism. Although the current resident population remains small, a goodly number of top-notch restaurants and inns have emerged in the Russian River Valley, catering to weekenders and summer vacationers.

More than sixty wineries may be discovered on the backroads of the Russian River Valley, where more than ten thousand acres of the broad alluvial gravel fans and low hills along the river have been planted to vineyards.

Wine aficionado or not, you will enjoy a slow mosey along what is known as the Russian River Wine Road. On Westside Road at the south end of the Dry Creek Valley, a wooden mill wheel turns at Mill Creek Vineyards, a small, family-owned winery that offers views of the valley, Fitch Mountain, and Mount St. Helena. Take a walk through a garden graced by an immense two-hundred-year-old oak and native plant species that were here back when Native Americans were the only residents. Have a picnic and taste the Kreck family's estate-bottled Chardonnays, Cabernets, and Zinfandels.

When you see three tall, connected, steep-roofed buildings, you've reached Hop Kiln Winery. The landmark triple hop kilns were built in 1905 by Italian stonemasons for drying hops, which were used to make beer. Known these days for spicy Zinfandels, the winery also produces "A Thousand Flowers," a summery combination of Chardonnay, Gewürztraminer, and Riesling, redolent of tropical fruit and green apple.

In the early 1970s, Davis Bynum Winery, just south on Westside Road, was the first to create a Russian River Valley Pinot Noir from a single vineyard. If you love the plumy, raspberry, black-cherry flavors of gentle tannin Pinots, stop for the reserve wines sold only here at the winery.

Where Westside Road meets California Highway 116 at Guerneville, the river begins to slow and widen, in anticipation of its final release at the Pacific Ocean. Foothills become mountains, oaks give way to dark redwood and fir forests, and the roadsides turn ferny and damp. Morning and evening fogs roll off the sea and up the river into the valley, cooling the rich, black clay soils and helping to create the famous fruit-intense, elegant Chardonnays, Pinots, and Merlots of the Russian River appellation. In the middle of the county, the AVA borders both sides of the river for over a hundred miles.

Settled in 1865 by loggers, Guerneville boomed when the railroad hauled out tons of redwood lumber used to build San Francisco. The visitors' center at what is now Korbel Champagne Cellars was once a train station. Korbel was founded in 1882 by Czech immigrants, who built the massive, ivy-covered stone replica of a Bohemian tower that you see today. The guided tour here is among the most complete of all California wineries and includes a museum, a film, an in-depth explanation of classic *méthode champenoise* production, and a tasting of bubbly. Save a half-hour or so to stroll the gardens—hundreds of antique rose bushes, spring-blooming bulbs, and a rare redwood hedge that encircle the Victorian-era house.

When you stop in Guerneville, enjoy a meal or take a swim at one of the sandy beaches, which have lifeguards in summertime. Visitors from the San Francisco Bay Area have long gathered in the Guerneville area to attend the Russian River Jazz Festival at Johnson Beach in September, the best month of the year for crystalline-clear, warm days and nights. Some travelers take their rest in the Applewood Inn, which offers luxury unexpected in this rustic corner of the county.

From downtown Guerneville, take Armstrong Woods Road into Armstrong Redwoods State Reserve for walks in the eight hundred acres of redwood groves on Fife Creek. Easy footpaths lead to centuries-old trees hundreds of feet tall. The Parson Jones Tree is over three hundred feet tall—longer than the length of a football field. Named for the lumberman who set the groves aside for public use in the 1870s, the Colonel Armstrong

*Winemaker Frank Hasek, seen here straddling a barrel of bubbly in 1896, was brought over from Prague by the Korbel family to produce champagne-style wines. (Courtesy Korbel Champagne Cellars)*

*Originally built for drying hops for beer, the main building at Hop Kiln Winery is a California Registered Historical Landmark.*

**CLOCKWISE FROM TOP:**
*The sunset sky provides yet another hue above the rainbow of reds, yellows, and greens at the Foppiano Vineyards in autumn.*

*A popular recreation destination in summer, the Russian River also brings the cool ocean air to the valley's many vineyards.*

*A stream rushes through the Austin Creek Recreation Area.*

Tree is at least 1,400 years old. A less-developed, adjacent preserve, Austin Creek Recreation Area, spreads out in thousands of acres of canyons and river glens that campers, hikers, and horseback riders love to explore. Anglers head to Redwood Lake for the bluegill and black bass.

Past Guerneville a few miles, bear right into the tiny Villa Grande, a river-bend village that looks as it did in the 1920s, when it was a summer encampment for San Franciscans flush enough to have second homes. Most tourists never find the hidden beaches here and the delightful array of early California Craftsman–style cottages.

Another of the old villages along the river, Duncans Mills is a cluster of galleries, cafés, shops, a campground, and the only remaining North Pacific Gauge Railroad station, now a museum.

## GREEN VALLEY SHANGRI-LA
### KINGDOM OF PINOT NOIR

### ROUTE 8
From U.S. Highway 101 north of Santa Rosa, take River Road west. Go south on Martinelli Road and northwest on California Highway 116. Head south on Green Valley Road and Harrison Grade Road, then east on Graton Road. Go north on Highway 116 to Forestville, taking a sidetrip on Ross Station Road along the way.

The adventurous spirit discovers the secrets of Green Valley, an often overlooked triangle of the Russian River Valley between Sebastopol, Occidental, and Guerneville. Misted by the nearby Pacific Ocean, gloomy redwood groves live in rocky canyons and creekbeds and march across wild, windy, hilltop ridges. Ocean fogs drift in through the "Petaluma Gap," remaining longer here than in the rest of the river valley and causing long hang times and later harvests than in most California grape-growing regions.

Below lines of low hills, spreading like rivulets on either side of the Russian, vineyards and orchards dominate the landscape in a microclimate perfectly suited to the growing of apples, plums, and wine grapes known for their singular character. The Farmhouse Inn and Restaurant on River Road is a classic American farmhouse, built in 1873 and owned by the Bartolomei family since the turn of the twentieth century. Inside, a mural painted by local artist Alice Thibault depicts the halcyon early days of western Sonoma County, long before the wine industry transformed the diverse agricultural economy and the way of life.

In this AVA, the noble burgundy grape, Pinot Noir, is king. The grape is notoriously difficult and expensive to grow because of the dangerous powdery mildew in the cool, moist climates where it is grows best, and due to the grape's thin skin, which is susceptible to splitting in the rain. Pinot Noir grapes produce vastly different styles of wine depending upon the plot of ground on which they are grown. Green Valley Pinots are known to be fruitier, having somewhat less minerality than most Pinots, low tannins, and relatively high acid levels for a red grape. Words used to describe Green Valley Pinots are lyrical—*buttery bing cherry*, *dark fruit*, *pomegranate*, *spicy cherry*, *spicy cola*, *cinnamon*, and *clove*. Sometimes these Pinots have an earthiness like the smell and taste of mushrooms, but above all, they are characterized by an exceedingly long finish. And therein lies the fame and fortune of Green Valley.

The Pinots of Hartford Family Winery are made from grapes grown in the Arrendell vineyard, a patch of land off Martinelli Road that is said to be the chilliest in the valley; harvest often does not occur there until the end of October. Hartford's ruby-hued Pinots have complex aromas of red raspberries, cherry jam, smoke, and spice.

Named for an old winemaking family, Martinelli Road is one of the loveliest lanes in California. A forest of redwoods, bays, and maples is the backdrop for split-rail fences and vintage farmhouses. The Martinelli Vineyard, and the Jackass Hill Vineyard on the hillside above, have been owned by the Martinelli family since the late 1800s. Five generations have worked together to produce their apples and their wines. Martinelli Vineyards welcomes visitors to a historic, red hop barn on River Road, where Muscat the cat holds court in a retail shop crowded with old-fashioned china and trinkets.

Chardonnay and Pinot Noir are created with Spanish flair at Marimar Torres Estate Winery on Graton Road. Marimar Torres is descended from the House of Torres, a Spanish family that has made wine since the 1870s and is today the largest independent producer in Spain. Torres planted her Green Valley Chardonnay and Pinot Noir vineyards in an extremely dense European style—two thousand vines per acre, over four times the normal density in California. The organically farmed vines are also trained quite low to the ground, in order to receive warmth from the earth and protection from the sun. The result of these techniques is low yields of fruit with concentrated aromas and flavors. In a tile-roofed, golden-toned hacienda on a hilltop, the winery resembles an elegant Catalan farmhouse, decorated inside with antiques and ceramics from Spain.

A narrow, oak-lined byway, Ross Station Road crosses a bridge and coils up a hill to a spectacular view of the Green Valley, the Sonoma and Mayacamas ranges, and Mount St. Helena. At the end of the road on the grounds of Iron Horse Ranch and Vineyards, palm and olive trees and stepped gardens surround the restored 1876 Carpenter Gothic family home of the winery owners, the Sterlings. Iron Horse sparkling wines have been served at state dinners in the Reagan, Clinton, and both Bush White Houses.

Although gradually encroached upon by the vineyards of premium wineries and grape growers, a handful of orchards in Green Valley still produce the pale red-and-green-striped Gravenstein apple, now considered an heirloom variety and beloved for the making of pies and applesauce. Until the last quarter of the twentieth century, the Green Valley area was called the "Gravenstein Apple Capital of the World." Today, the remaining produce farmers grow primarily modern apple varieties, as well as blueberries, olallieberries, and other fruits. Berries, artisan cheeses, olive oils, nuts, and other locally produced foodstuffs are for sale, along with pies, ciders, and jams, at weekend farmers' markets and roadside stands and at the annual Apple Blossom Festival that takes place in Sebastopol in April.

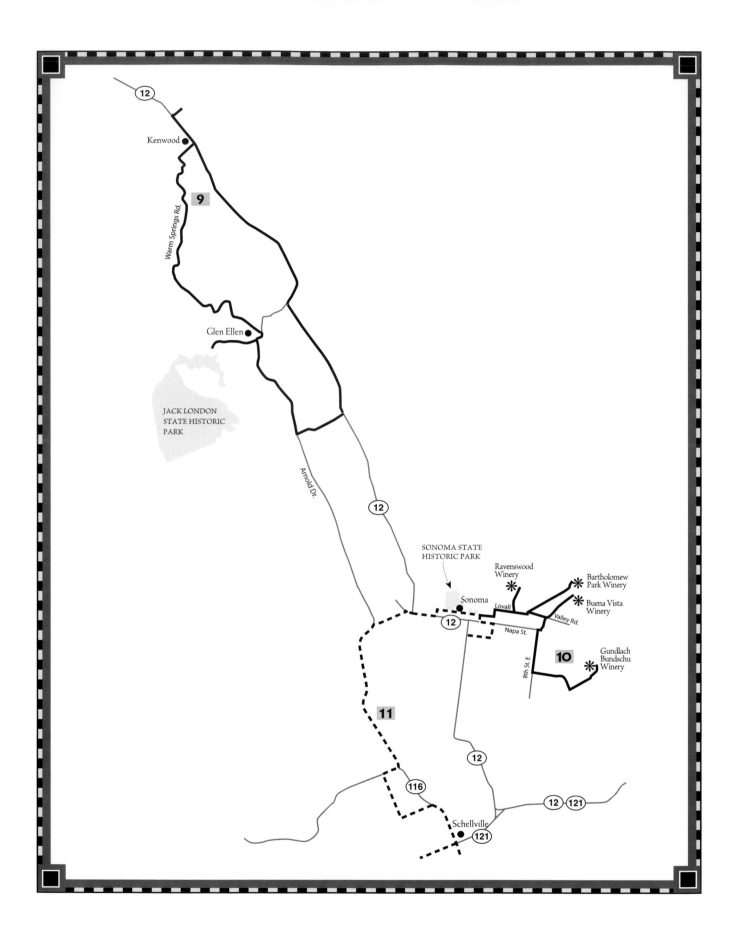

12

Kenwood •

*Warm Springs Rd.*

**9**

Glen Ellen •

JACK LONDON
STATE HISTORIC
PARK

*Arnold Dr.*

12

SONOMA STATE
HISTORIC PARK

Sonoma •

Ravenswood
Winery ✴

Bartholomew
Park Winery ✴

Buena Vista
Winery ✴

*Lovall*

*Valley Rd.*

Napa St.

12

*8th St. E*

**10**

Gundlach
Bundschu
Winery ✴

**11**

12

116

12   121

Schellville •   121

Born in San Francisco in 1876, the son of an itinerant astrologer/journalist and a spiritualist, Jack London hung around the Oakland docks as a teenager, taking up with a gang of oyster pirates on the bay. He sailed to Japan and the Bering Sea as a seventeen-year-old seaman and came home to write his first published story, "Typhoon Off the Coast of Japan."

After joining the Socialist Labor Party, London wandered around the United States, got arrested for vagrancy in New York, and explored the Klondike for gold in 1897, always writing. His adventure novel, *The Call of the Wild*, was published in 1903, catapulting him into public notice and enabling him to purchase his "Beauty Ranch" on the west side of the Sonoma Valley. Interrupting his orchard and vineyard planting and homebuilding, he and his wife, Charmian, set off for what they intended to be a round-the-world voyage on the *Snark*, a fifty-five-foot yacht built in San Francisco. They sailed to Hawaii, the Marquesas Islands, Tahiti, and the Solomon Islands, ending the trip on the island of Guadalcanal, where Jack became ill and decided to return home. He continued to write, producing more than fifty books, including *White Fang*, *South Sea Tales*, and *The Sea Wolf*, as well as many articles. He made wine, husbanded pigs and other farm animals, rode horses around the ranch, and drank a lot.

After his death of kidney disease at age forty in 1916, Charmian built the Spanish-tile-roofed, fieldstone-walled "House of Happy Walls," which is now a museum in Jack London State Historic Park. Original furnishings, photographs, souvenirs from world travels, London's roll-top desk and Dictaphone, and even rejection slips from publishers, create a poignant scene.

Jack London wrote of Sonoma County, "The air is wine. Across Sonoma Mountain, wisps of sea fog are stealing. The afternoon sun smolders in the drowsy sky. I have everything to make me glad I am alive."

*The Jack London Bookstore in Glen Ellen, near Jack London State Historic Park, celebrates the work of this California favorite son.*

## VALLEY OF THE MOON
### CALL OF THE WILD

A few stone and clapboard buildings from the late 1800s, mossy oaks hanging over a creek, and a handful of cafés huddle on one meandering road at the foot of a deeply forested mountain. The tiny village of Glen Ellen seems lost in time—lost in Jack London's time, early in the twentieth century, when he wrote the classic adventure tales *The Call of the Wild* and *The Sea Wolf*. London loved roaming his sprawling ranch here in the wild hills of Sonoma County. He wrote about the area in his 1913 novel *The Valley of the Moon*, taking the title from the Pomo and Miwok Indian words for Sonoma, "valley of many moons."

London grew grapes and made his own wine in what is today the Sonoma Mountain appellation. High above the Sonoma Valley, his home ranch

### ROUTE 9

From Glen Ellen, take London Ranch Road to Jack London State Historic Park and back; then drive northwest on Warm Springs Road to Kenwood. In Kenwood, head about 0.8 mile north on California Highway 12 to reach Chateau St. Jean. Head south on Highway 12 to Madrone Road. Turn west on Madrone Road and take Arnold Drive north to return to Glen Ellen.

**FACING PAGE, TOP:**
The mansion at Chateau St. Jean was built by a Michigan mining magnate in 1920. The grounds feature fishponds in the shape of Lakes Michigan and Huron.

**FACING PAGE, BOTTOM:**
In addition to the grapes grown on the winery's own twenty-two acres, Kenwood Vineyards produces wines using grapes from throughout Sonoma County.

**ABOVE:**
Jack London began building his dream house on his 1,500-acre Beauty Ranch in 1911, but a fire two years later brought the project to a premature end. Today, the Wolf House is part of the Jack London State Historic Park.

**LEFT:**
Oak trees provide cooling shade at Glen Ellen's Sonoma Valley Regional Park.

is now Jack London State Historic Park, consisting of about a thousand acres of hiking and horseback riding trails; groves of oaks, madrones, Douglas firs, and redwoods; and wildflower meadows. Most visitors take the short walk to the haunting ruins of Wolf House, London's massive stone mansion that burned to the ground in 1913 a few days before he and his wife, Charmian, could move in. Remnants of a reflecting pool, long galleries, huge fireplaces, the bark-encrusted redwoods used for columns, and curving stone stairways remain.

Kenwood Vineyards owns the lava-terraced vineyards on the London ranch. Their Cabernets, Zinfandels, and Merlots are beloved for their minty, zesty, berry flavors. On their dramatic label is a replica of the wolf's head depicted on London's bookplates.

Chardonnay, Cabernet Sauvignon, Sauvignon Blanc, and Zinfandel grapes are the stars of the Sonoma Valley appellation; the mighty Cabs grow in the steady sunlight above the fog line, while other varieties are sheltered below, thriving in long growing seasons at lower temperatures. On London Ranch Road, Benziger Family Winery is situated in a vast volcanic bowl of sun-catching, terraced vineyards. Twenty-one types of soil have been identified on this property, which is particularly well suited to Cabernet grapes. Explore the demonstration vineyards here, hop on the open-air tram for a narrated ride through the vineyards, and spend time in the art gallery.

For decades, the Jack London Bookstore and Research Center in Glen Ellen has held forth in a ramshackle building crowded with London memorabilia and old books. When the shop is closed, choose your books from the bookshelves outside under the overhang and leave your money in the box.

Across the road, a burbling branch of Sonoma Creek turns an old gristmill. Walk through the vine-covered arbor to the Olive Press, where you can watch fruit being pressed at the first public cooperative olive mill in the state. Small commercial growers and hobbyists with homegrown olives bring their harvests to the press, usually beginning in December. All year round, you can taste olive oils, tapenades, and vinegars, and browse for ceramics from Provence.

Just south around the corner from the press is a trailhead for the Sonoma Valley Regional Park, where a paved path follows the creek for a mile or so through an oak forest. Bike here and picnic, or set off on foot on the maze of hillside trails.

From Glen Ellen, Warm Springs Road loops northwest through some of the loveliest landscape in California to the tiny burg of Kenwood. Near California Highway 12, the Kenwood Depot, a little architectural gem in the Richardsonian Romanesque style, was a Southern Pacific train station from 1888 to 1936. Nearby Kenwood Plaza is a nice, little park fronting the white-steepled Kenwood Community Church, anchoring the community of vintage cottages as it has since 1888.

Just north on Highway 12, wine lovers make pilgrimages to Chateau St. Jean for its highly rated, vineyard-designated wines. Cinq Cépages—"Five Varieties"—was named one of the best wines in the world in 2003. Each of the components of this Bordeaux-style wine—Cabernet Sauvignon, Merlot, Cabernet Franc, Malbec, and Petit Verdot—is aged separately for two years in small French oak barrels before blending. Surrounding the 1920s-era mansion are formal gardens and a redwood-shaded picnic area, making Chateau St. Jean a pleasant stop.

Heading south toward Sonoma, watch for the Kenwood Inn and Spa, an ochre-colored, cloistered hostelry impersonating a weathered villa in Tuscany. Honeymooners and weekenders retire in walled garden courtyards, hiding away in sumptuous suites and indulging in wine-themed spa treatments—Merlot wraps, Cabernet scrubs, and bubbling wine-barrel baths.

On Madrone Road, Valley of the Moon Winery welcomes visitors into a nineteenth-century stone building on the creek side. Tall-paned windows frame the gardens and an old Zinfandel vineyard. A three-hundred-year-old bay tree stands in silent splendor, its bark, perhaps, infused with memories of when the first inhabitants of the valley gathered acorns and fished in the streams.

## THE SONOMA VALLEY
### OLD MISSION DAYS

Sonoma was settled in 1823 by Franciscan padre Jose Altimira, who planted the first grapevines here. He also built San Francisco Solano de Sonoma, the northernmost mission church on El Camino Real, the road that linked California's twenty-one Spanish missions. In the 1830s, Mexican general Mariano Vallejo laid out a small pueblo around the mission and built adobe barracks for his battalion of soldiers. Today the original plaza is bordered by the barracks, a few adobes, and the mission, plus a colorful collection of Western false-front buildings and fanciful Victorian mansions that now house shops and restaurants. A National Historic Landmark, and a beautiful one, the Sonoma plaza has huge bay and eucalyptus trees, a stream with chattering ducks, picnic tables on the lawns, and a monolithic stone city hall. The stone building was erected in 1908 with four identical sides, to satisfy merchants on all sides of the plaza.

Look for the flag-bearing settler in bronze, a memorial to the Bear Flag Rebellion. On a hot, dusty day in June 1846, a ragged band of American settlers rode into town to Vallejo's barracks, whereupon they took the general prisoner, hoisted a homemade flag, and declared California an independent republic. Some days later, Mexico gave up all claim to Alta California, and General Vallejo went on to become a state senator and, later, the mayor of Sonoma.

Sonomans are still proud of their rebellious attitudes and a certain laid-back, often humorous approach to the mystique of winemaking. Today, they live a wine-country lifestyle about which books are written. Above all, they are wine buffs and "foodies," appreciating the locally produced artisanal cheeses, specialty fruits and vegetables, and rustic breads that are sold at twice-weekly farmers' markets. Among the exceptional cheeses made in Sonoma are Vella's Bear Flag Dry Jack, the Sonoma Cheese Factory's lusciously soft Teleme, and Laura Chenel's famous goat cheeses, produced at her factory just east of town. Artisan Bakers' crusty sourdough loaves won the 1996 Coupe du Monde de la

ROUTE 10

From Sonoma Plaza, go east on East Spain Street, north on Fourth Street East, east on Lovall Valley Road, and north on Gehricke Road to Ravenswood Winery. Return to Lovall Valley Road heading east and go north on Castle Road and Vineyard Lane. Returning to Lovall Valley Road and continuing east, turn north onto Old Winery Road to Buena Vista Winery, then reverse direction and follow Eighth Street East south and Denmark Street east to Gundlach Bundschu Winery.

The property at Bartholomew Park Winery was first planted with grapes as early as the 1850s. The winery's Pompeian Villa reflects an even older tradition.

**LEFT:**
Above colorful murals, a worker tends to the wine tanks at Gundlach Bundschu Winery.

**FACING PAGE, CLOCKWISE FROM TOP LEFT:**
Elegant oak doors adorned with windows etched with the winery's logo welcome visitors to Ravenswood Winery in Sonoma.

Sonoma Overlook Trail offers an inviting hike through scenic landscapes with spectacular views of the Sonoma Valley.

The picnic area at Buena Vista Winery is an idyllic spot to sample wines while lunching in the fresh California air.

*This vintage postcard shows the underground tasting room at Sonoma's Buena Vista Vineyards.*

Boulangerie (World Cup of Baking) in Paris, a first for an American baker. The gourmet gadget store Williams-Sonoma was launched here, and renowned chefs from around the world teach classes at Ramekins Sonoma Valley Culinary School, in an adobe-like "rammed earth" building.

From the plaza, you can walk, bike, or drive on quiet, tree-shaded country roads to several historic wineries and drive to more than three dozen more in the valley. Morning fogs drifting in from San Pablo Bay and cooled airflows coming in over the Santa Rosa Plain from the Pacific balance hot summer and fall temperatures. Combined with well-drained, stony soils, the weather creates a distinctive *terroir* that produces wine grapes with concentrated, complex flavors, notably Cabernet Sauvignon, Merlot, Zinfandel, Chardonnay, and Italian varietals.

Stop at the Sebastiani Vineyards and Winery on Fourth Street East to experience a piece of winemaking history. In 1904, Samuele Sebastiani, who had come to California from Tuscany at age fourteen, acquired the original Spanish mission vineyards in Sonoma and built a stone winery that still stands today. Samuele's son, August, enlarged the winery a hundredfold in the 1940s. His introduction of "Nouveau" Gamay Beaujolais to the American market was a milestone in production, as the wine eventually sold millions of cases. When you visit Sebastiani Vineyards, notice the stained-glass window on the west side of the main, stone winery building; it depicts August Sebastiani in his signature wide-brimmed hat and overalls.

On a forested hillside a short walk from the plaza, Ravenswood Winery is best known for Zinfandel. You get a close-up view of its postcard-perfect vineyards by walking up Gehricke Road under mossy oaks and past creeks, canyons, and rolling hills. Ravenswood is popular on weekends for its "Barbecue in the Vineyards," taking place on the winery's shady terrace. The event features homemade sausages and the Ravenous Burger, washed down with the winery's hearty reds. The Ravenswood motto: "No Wimpy Wines."

An allée of trees leads to the end of Castle Road and Bartholomew Park Winery, where stands a reconstruction of a rather peculiar Pompeian villa, built in the mid-nineteenth century by a Hungarian count, Agoston Haraszthy. Just beyond, a Spanish-Colonial-style building houses a tasting room, museum, and photography gallery. One of the nicest picnic grounds at any California winery, the Wine Garden lies beneath a canopy of oaks. From here, hiking trails loop around the foothills and meadows that are replete with wildflowers in the spring.

From here, walk or drive to the enchanted gardens and vine-covered stone buildings of Buena Vista Winery, which was founded in 1857 by Count Haraszthy. A natural salesman, he convinced the state to pay for a trip to Europe, where he collected a hundred thousand vinifera cuttings. He returned to dole them out to fledgling local growers and plant his own vineyards. A genius at grape growing and winemaking, Haraszthy shared his knowledge widely and is known as the father of California viticulture. Always a notorious character, he disappeared in 1869 at age fifty-seven while on a trip to Nicaragua, and there is reason to believe he was gobbled up by a crocodile.

Bright with art and antiques, Buena Vista's tasting room in the original stone press house is shaded by a grove of oaks, beneath which picnickers linger over bottles of medal-winning Cabernets, Pinot Noirs, and Chardonnays. Bring your camera to shoot the huge carved wine barrel and other artifacts of early winemaking.

Continue your tour on the backroads to Gundlach Bundschu Winery. A fortune seeker during the California Gold Rush, Jacob Gundlach sailed to San Francisco in 1851 and moved to the Sonoma Valley in 1858 to develop his Rhine-style farm, where he plowed, behind a horse, the first Johannesburg Riesling vineyards in the state. His great-great-grandson, Jim Bundschu, and Jim's sons now run the winery, which continues to produce German varietals and estate-grown Merlots, Pinots, and Cabernets. There are oak-shaded picnic grounds here and, in the summertime, an outdoor stage where Shakespearean plays are performed.

## GATEWAY TO SONOMA VALLEY
### ITALIAN HERITAGE AND THE GENERAL'S HOUSE

Dropping into the Sonoma Valley on gently rolling hills, vineyards and meadowy pastures stretch to the rugged Mayacamas Mountains in the east and to the lower Sonoma Mountains in the west. Seven miles wide and seventeen miles long, the Sonoma Valley is a landscape reminiscent of the Mediterranean and primarily devoted to agriculture and oak woodlands.

Located at the end of an olive- and cypress-lined drive like a villa in Tuscany, Viansa Winery and Italian Marketplace commands a hill above California Highway 121. In the colorful marketplace, pick up picnic items to eat at tables under the trees, and shop for packaged foodstuffs, cookbooks, and Italian-made ceramics. In addition to traditional California varietals, Sangiovese, Vernaccia, Nebbiolo, Aleatico, and Trebbiano are some of the lesser-known grapes blended into the Viansa wines.

From the terrace at Viansa Winery, you will get tremendous views of the north end of San Francisco Bay and ninety acres of vast wetlands. Winery co-owner Sam Sebastiani, a member of the prominent Sonoma winemaking family, has restored one of the largest private waterfowl preserves in the state, an important stop for ducks and geese that migrate from Canada and Alaska to Mexico on the Pacific flyway. More than ten thousand birds have been spotted here on a winter day.

From your vantage point high above the south end of the Sonoma Valley, you may spy a bright-red biplane zooming about from the nearby roadside airfield, Aeroschellville. You may wish to spend an hour at the airfield, looking

ROUTE 11

From the junction of California Highway 37 and California Highway 121, drive north on Highway 121 to Schellville. At the intersection of California Highways 121 and 116, drive west on Bonneau Road to Schug Carneros Estate Winery, then return to Highway 116 and continue north. Go west on East Bonness Road, then north on Bonness Road, which will lead you back to Highway 116. Follow Highway 116 east and drive north on Arnold Drive to Petaluma Avenue. Go east on Petaluma Avenue into Sonoma and continue east on West Napa Street. Take West Fifth Street north and West Spain Street east into Sonoma's east-side neighborhoods.

No, you haven't been transported to the hills of Catalonia, Spain. That's the Gloria Ferrer Champagne Caves winery, one of California's premier producers of sparkling wines.

Among the innovative, rotating displays at the Cornerstone Festival of Gardens is this "Small Tribute to Immigrant Workers," designed by Mario Schjetnan of Mexico City.

**ABOVE:**
In addition to its impressive legacy of Sonoma Valley wines, the Sebastiani family also built this elegant movie house in downtown Sonoma in 1933.

**LEFT:**
Serving local dishes with a southwestern influence, the General's Daughter Restaurant is a fine place to sample classic wine country fare.

*The interior of the General M. G. Vallejo Home appears more or less as it did 150 years ago.*

at the World War II–era, and earlier, models, including a rare Navy SNJ-4 trainer. Take a soothing, soundless sightseeing ride in a glider, or go for loops and rolls in the open cockpit of a 1940 Stearman.

You cannot miss the blue tree on the side of the road at the Cornerstone Festival of Gardens. Unique in the United States, the gardens are a gallery of whimsical—some say odd—landscape displays, from a forest of red bamboo poles to boulder gardens, Asian-inspired minimalist installations, and more.

In the western foothills, the Gloria Ferrer Champagne Caves float above the valley like a mirage of a Spanish hacienda. Built by the largest sparkling-wine company in the world, Freixenet of Spain, Ferrer is the perfect venue for Catalan cooking classes, Flamenco shows, and other cultural events throughout the year.

After arriving at Schellville, which consists of an intersection with a gas station and a motel, go west on Bonneau Road if you are a Pinot Noir lover or a photographer. It will take you through an ocean of vines to Schug Carneros Estate Winery, a German-style, post-and-beam winery tucked up against the low range of hills. Owner and winemaster Walter Schug was raised in Germany's Rhine River valley on a Pinot Noir estate. Infused with a fresh, concentrated berry character, his Pinots are medal winners, as are his full-bodied Chardonnays. From the road just below the winery are wide views of the Sonoma Valley and, on clear days, San Francisco Bay.

North America's first winery established by a Mexican migrant worker is a delightful stop on Bonness Road. Reynado Robledo, the patriarch of the Robledo Family Winery, founded in 1997, came to California from Michoacan as a sixteen-year-old and initially worked as a vine pruner at Christian Brothers Winery in the Napa Valley. Today, seven sons and two daughters are involved in the business, while a son-in-law, Rolando Herrera, crafts the award-winning Robledo wines. The winery hosts an annual harvest festival in October when a mariachi band and folkloric dancers joyously evoke the spirit of Michoacan.

There are simple pleasures to be found on Arnold Drive. At the stoplight at Watmaugh Road is a strawberry stand, open half of the year, where just-picked berries are piled in baskets moments before your arrival. Watch for vibrant murals on the outside of Juanita Juanita, a tiny, mighty Mexican restaurant that is rated the best by Mexico-born locals.

In the town of Sonoma, on West Spain Street, look for the big, mustard yellow Victorian mansion that is The General's Daughter restaurant. The mansion was built in 1864 by Mexican general Mariano Vallejo for his daughter Natalia. Near the restaurant is the eucalyptus-lined entrance to the General M. G. Vallejo Home, or Lachryma Montis ("Tears of the Mountain"), which is now part of the Sonoma State Historic Park. The classic, Yankee-style, yellow and white Gothic Revival house was shipped around South America's Cape Horn in pieces and erected in 1851. Original and period furnishings, including marble fireplaces, tin bathtubs, lace coverlets, and cut-velvet couches, re-create the days when Vallejo and his family lived here. When not monitoring his small army, Vallejo planted orchards and vineyards and engaged in friendly winemaking competition with other vintners. In the carriage house museum here, look for the silver berry spoon that was presented to the general for being "Maker of Best Red Wine 1858."

*General Mariano Vallejo, shown here with a few of his daughters and granddaughters, built his home on a large land grant in the heart of California's wine-growing region.*

You can stroll the lovely gardens at the Vallejo home and walk right onto a paved trail that traces the north edge of the town of Sonoma. The trail meanders between playing fields and a marshy meadow where red-winged blackbirds fly and herons hide. Along the trail in Depot Park is a small history museum and a well-used court for petanque (a game similar to bocce ball). Walking east on the path you will pass The Patch, a vegetable stand beside a huge garden, where corn, tomatoes, and other produce are picked fresh every day in season. The Vella Cheese Company sits across the street in a turn-of-the-nineteenth-century brick brewery building. The company is one of the oldest cheesemakers in the state and the developer of Dry Jack and other singular varieties.

To complete your exploration of Sonoma, walk south on the sidewalks of the "Eastside" to see an idyllic neighborhood of old gardens, magnificent trees, and architecture from many eras—from thick-walled adobes to Victorian mansions to California Craftsman bungalows.

# PART III

# NAPA VALLEY:
# HEART OF THE WINE COUNTRY

**FACING PAGE:**
*The backroads of the Napa Valley zigzag past hundreds of scenic vineyards.*

**ABOVE:**
*This statue of a wine presser greets visitors to Napa Valley wine country.*

In his autobiography, *Harvests of Joy*, Robert Mondavi wrote, "Wine to me is passion. It's family and friends. It's warmth of heart and generosity of spirit. Wine is art. It's culture. It's the essence of civilization and the art of living."

Thanks to Mondavi and other visionaries who promote the Napa wine world, nowhere else in California does the art of living seem to be as highly cultivated and as prized as it is here. Millions of visitors arrive annually to partake of the grape, the legendary restaurants, and the mild, Mediterranean weather. Nonetheless, you can still get lost on lonely backroads, and you can still discover small, little-known, family-operated wineries.

From the town of Napa north to Calistoga, the thirty-mile-long Napa Valley is crisscrossed by quiet country roads, which provide respite from the busy main thoroughfares of California Highway 29 and the Silverado Trail. More than a dozen crossroads offer quiet biking and walking routes, glimpses of winery estates, and unobstructed views of vineyards stretching across the valley floor.

Of all the California wine valleys, the landscape and the climate here is most reminiscent of southern Italy and France. One-sixth the size of Bordeaux, the Napa Valley is oriented north-south. The lower end is open to the cool fogs and breezes of San Francisco Bay, and the upper end is hot and dry. The wide variety of soil types create a myriad of *terroirs* on dry, rocky hillsides; on the loamy valley floor along the Napa River; and on the benchlands, triangular alluvial fans of gravelly deposits eroded down from the mountains.

On the valley floor, four picturesque small towns are headquarters for forays to hot springs spas, historic sites, walking and biking trails along the river, and more than 240 wineries. The Napa Valley is home to more premium wineries than anywhere in North America.

Expeditions up serpentine tracks into the two mountain ranges that rim the valley will lead you through dark, primordial forests, wild, rocky canyons, and what's left of the rough-and-tumble towns founded during the 1800s. Among the cow and horse pastures and the oak woodlands, vineyards cascade over stony terraces, struggling to thrive at high altitudes and in low temperatures. Stopping along the way to tour and taste at the scattering of wineries off the beaten track, you will discover that the more difficult the growing conditions, the more concentrated and complex the flavors and the character of the wines. So what if you do get lost?

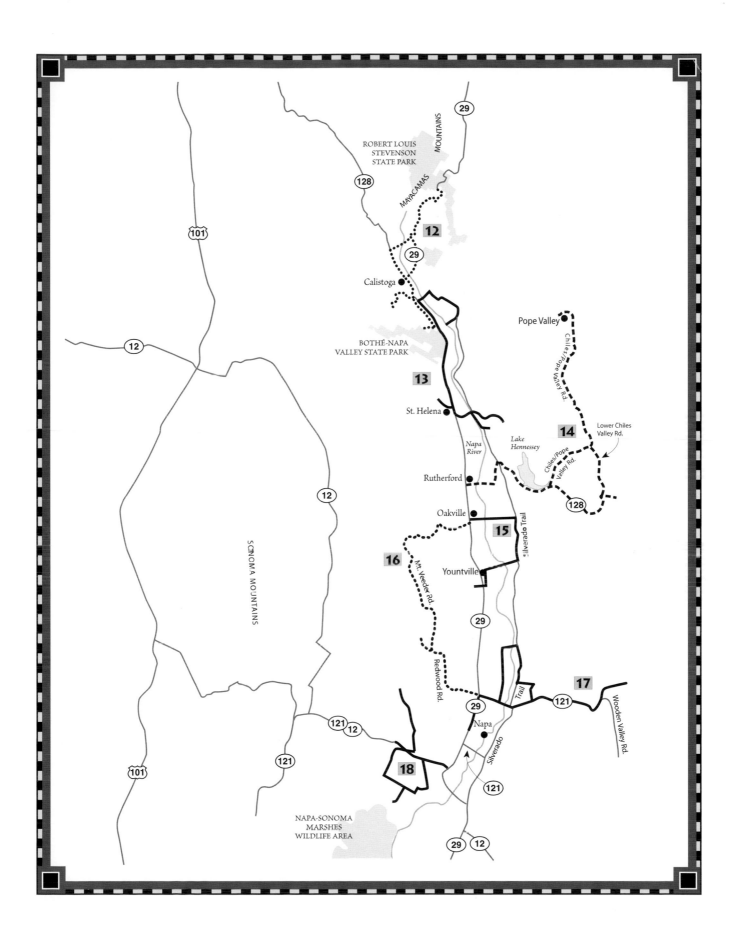

**TOP:**
*Wine-country travelers gather in the pre-dawn hours for a thrilling trip over the valley by hot-air balloon.*

**ABOVE:**
*Morning fog creeps in behind the historic winery building at Ehlers Estate, built in 1886.*

**RIGHT:**
*Just thirty miles long, the world-famous Napa Valley region is home to more than 250 wineries.*

**FACING PAGE:**
*A rainbow forms amidst a clearing spring storm over vineyards along Conn Valley Road.*

**LEFT:**
*The 1883 Rhine House at the Beringer Vineyard brings the family's German heritage to sunny California.*

**BELOW:**
*The Napa River flows below an old stone bridge near St. Helena.*

# ST. HELENA
## A VICTORIAN TOWN AND HIDDEN VALLEYS

### ROUTE 13

Start at Joseph Phelps Vineyard on Taplin Road, off the Silverado Trail. Proceed north on the Trail to Howell Mountain Road, which runs east to Meadowood Lane and Conn Valley Road. Return to the Trail, go west on Pope Street then north on California Highway 29 through St. Helena. Drive west on Madrona Street and north on Spring Mountain Road. Back on Highway 29, go north to Dunaweal Lane, which runs northeast to the Silverado Trail. Follow the Trail south and head west on Larkmead Lane to Frank Family Vineyards.

Nearly the entire Napa Valley between California Highway 29 and the Silverado Trail is crisscrossed by short roads, each of which rambles between endless vineyards and past glorious old mansions and wineries. Along the east side of the Silverado Trail in the rugged foothills of the Vaca Range, wineries, a few inns, and lovely, lonely country roads are discoveries to be made.

In idyllic Spring Valley, Joseph Phelps Vineyards offers one of the most in-depth, sophisticated wine tasting and educational programs in the valley. Plan to settle in here for an hour or so. An innovator since the winery's founding in 1972, Joseph Phelps introduced Insignia, the first Bordeaux-style blend produced in California under a proprietary label; one of the first of the California-style Syrahs; and an entire family of Rhône-style wines, including a Châteauneuf-du-Pape–type blend called Le Mistral. If you decide to picnic under the oaks, a staff member will pair the perfect bottle of wine with your menu.

Take a sidetrip through lush countryside on twisting and turning Conn Valley Road to Conn Valley Vineyards, where one of the Anderson family will likely climb off a tractor and welcome you to taste Cabernet Sauvignon in the cool caves. Before returning to the Silverado Trail, stop in at Meadowood, a posh, 1920s-style, wisteria-draped country lodge in a riparian forest on Meadowood Lane. Residing regally on a rise overlooking the woods, the resort is the home of the annual Napa Valley Wine Auction, a four-day event attended by deep-pocket bidders and wine lovers from around the world.

The town of St. Helena is postcard perfect with old-fashioned streetlights on tree-shaded streets lined with Victorian houses and steepled churches. An old-fashioned gazebo, and a fountain just for dogs and horses, are found in the tiny town park on Main Street. At the Robert Louis Stevenson Museum, thousands of pieces of the author's memorabilia are displayed, while next door the Napa Valley Wine Library houses a myriad of reference materials on the art of winemaking and the history of the valley.

Heading west into the Mayacamas Range from St. Helena, Spring Mountain Road is a narrow track of hairpin turns and switchbacks promising a slow journey through some the wildest Napa and Sonoma County terrain. In the fall, big leaf maples and oaks turn the entire forest into a red and gold cathedral, as vivid as New England in October.

In the Spring Mountain viticultural area, you will encounter several small premium wineries. At two thousand feet in elevation, above the fog line in thin, rocky soil, Ritchie Creek Vineyard produces fewer than a thousand cases of deeply concentrated Cabernets and other wines per year. A glorious garden terrace at Schweiger Vineyard is the place to sip some Cabernet and drink in stunning mountain and valley views.

Driving north from St. Helena, you will see redwood forests grow darker and deeper. Watch for Beringer Vineyard's Rhine House, built in 1883 as a

The Christian Brothers Monastery and Vineyards
Mont La Salle, Napa County, California

tribute to the founder's family home in Germany. This house is a good place to take a full winery tour, as it includes huge cellar caves carved into the hillside by Chinese laborers in the nineteenth century.

Just beyond Beringer is Greystone, the former Christian Brothers Winery, built in 1889 with twenty-two-inch-thick, hand-cut, volcanic stone blocks. Today Greystone houses the West Coast annex of the prestigious culinary college, the Culinary Institute of America (CIA). Visitors interested in fine food and wine-country history like to browse in the gourmet store and the food and wine museum, and enjoy regional and Mediterranean cuisine in the Wine Spectator Greystone Restaurant.

For a walk in the woods, Bothé-Napa Valley State Park makes a nice retreat, where footpaths and equestrian trails meander among stands of coastal redwoods, firs, and oaks. A short walk leads you to the adjacent Bale Grist Mill State Historic Park, a shady glade where a thirty-six-foot-tall grinding wheel is powered by a rushing creek.

North up the highway on Dunaweal Lane, Sterling Vineyards is a dazzling white, modern, Greek-island-style fortress on a high plateau, accessed by an aerial tram. Its sky-high terrace affords 360-degree valley views, as well as a sunny spot to picnic and taste their toasty, lemony Winery Lake Chardonnay.

Wine meets art at Clos Pegase, a russet-colored, postmodernist extravaganza of a winery, the result of an international architectural competi-

*The former Christian Brothers Monastery and Vineyards is now owned and operated by the CIA— the Culinary Institute of America.*

**ABOVE:**
*The stone winery and patio areas in rolling countryside give the Kuleto Estate Winery a truly Tuscan appeal.*

**RIGHT:**
*The Nichelini Winery has been making wines since 1884, although the old Roman wine press probably hasn't seen much use during that time.*

ABOVE:
*Combining the region's wine-making tradition with an Old West flavor, RustRidge Ranch and Winery is a uniquely Californian winery.*

tion. Besides wine tasting, you will find sculpture by world-famous artists, including Jean Dubuffet, Henry Moore, Mark di Suvero, and Richard Serra.

On Larkmead Lane, giant oak trees and a massive, golden sandstone winery mark Frank Family Vineyards, where Rich Frank, a former head of Walt Disney Studios, and his family make sparkling wine, Zinfandel port, Cabernet, and Chardonnay. While you are here, take a look at the Marilyn Monroe memorabilia and the Frank's collection of vintage autos.

## EASTERN NAPA VALLEY
### RUTHERFORD TO POPE VALLEY AND THE LAKE

ROUTE 14

From California Highway 29 at Rutherford, drive east on Rutherford Road then north on Conn Creek Road to the Silverado Trail. Follow Sage Canyon Road/California Highway 128 east and make a left turn onto Lower Chiles Valley Road, heading north to Pope Valley Road to Pope Valley. Reverse direction, take a right turn south onto Chiles/Pope Valley Road, and return to Sage Canyon Road.

A springtime drive in the mountains and wild valleys of eastern Napa County is a dream of Irish-green meadows vivid with wildflowers. Still part of the Napa Valley viticultural area, this backcountry area is sprinkled with a handful of small, historic wineries and a few newcomers. At an elevation of one thousand feet, and enjoying warmer days and cooler nights than the floor of the Napa Valley, the skinny Chiles Valley has a legacy of grape growing, primarily Cabernet Sauvignon, Merlot, Sauvignon Blanc, and Zinfandel varietals.

Sage Canyon Road borders the south side of Lake Hennessey, a reservoir where boating and trout and bass fishing are popular. Past the lake, continue to Kuleto Estate. Here, Pat Kuleto, a designer of flamboyant and highly successful restaurants, has built a rustic, Tuscan-style winery of stone, hand-hewn beams, and fancy ironwork. Sampling a Kuleto Syrah, Pinot Noir, or Sangiovese while sitting in an Adirondack chair on the stone patio, high above Lake Hennessey, it is easy to dream of the wine-country lifestyle.

Also on Sage Canyon Road, Nichelini Winery is a rustic, barnlike place that was homesteaded and hand-built in 1890 by Anton Nichelini, a Swiss-Italian immigrant. His grandchildren now operate the winery. After paying homage to the guard cat, Boots, take time to notice the rare, ancient Roman grape press and the stonework on the winery and the cellar. The reds under the Nichelini labels include Cabernets and a spicy old-vine Zinfandel with the aromas of cherries, anise, and chocolate. Delightful on a hot summer day is the Swiss-style Sauvignon Vert, vinted from grapes harvested from a 1946 planting.

Follow a loop north on Lower Chiles Valley Road, a narrow, corkscrew track rising to one thousand feet above sea level. At RustRidge Ranch and Winery, the tasting bar in a converted hay barn is surrounded by the activity of making Cabernets, Chardonnays, and Zinfandels. The yellow labs, Tosca and Charlie, will show you around the ranch, part of a Spanish land grant called Rancho Catacoula that was given to Colonel Joseph B. Chiles in 1844. The 1940s ranch house is now a bed-and-breakfast inn where guests enjoy swimming ponds, a tennis court, and hiking trails. In the house is a large collection of fascinating memorabilia related to Seabiscuit, the legendary racehorse, who winery co-owner Jim Fresquez worked with during his days as a trainer.

So revered that an official society was founded to extol its virtues, Rutherford Dust is the cocoa-colored soil in which wine grapes are grown in the Rutherford viticultural area, the oldest grape-growing district in the Napa Valley.

Bisected by California Highway 29—certainly not one of the backroads—this three-by-two-mile patch is the historic heart of the valley. The young Finnish fur trader, Captain Gustave Niebaum, arrived here in 1880 to purchase vineyard property and build a massive stone winery, Inglenook, seven years later. When a French émigré, Georges de Latour, planted the Beaulieu vineyards in 1900, a veritable winemaking boom was on. Nearly the entire three thousand acres between Oakville and the south border of St. Helena were planted with grapevines. As early as the mid-1890s, a half-million gallons of wine were being shipped annually to the East, the Midwest, and the cellars of San Francisco.

A vine pest, phylloxera, and Prohibition shut down winemaking in the area between 1920 and 1933. When Prohibition was repealed, vintner Louis Martini celebrated by sounding his winery's steam whistle long and loudly. Today, his granddaughter is the president of the Louis M. Martini winery in Rutherford.

The savior of the post-Prohibition Napa wine industry was Andre Tchelistcheff, a Russian-born resident of France who came on the scene in 1938. He spent his life experimenting with premium winemaking and teaching vintners and winemakers. It was Tchelistcheff who coined the term "Rutherford Dust," a certain *terroir* comprising diverse soil types and unique mesoclimates within the appellation. Some of most highly rated Cabernets from California are grown on the legendary Rutherford benches, three alluvial fans spreading down from the slopes of Mount St. John on the west and the Vaca Range on the east to the Napa River. The gravelly, sandy, and sometimes loamy soil is the Rutherford Dust.

In 1939, Georges de Latour's Cabernet Sauvignon won a gold medal at the Golden Gate International Exposition in San Francisco, and it was served at the White House in the 1940s. Since then, the Beaulieu Cabernets have remained the standard for Rutherford Cabs produced by the thirty or so contemporary wineries in the AVA.

At the turn of the twentieth century, the Pope Valley blacksmith founded the Burgundy Winery and Olive Factory, which was operated, except during Prohibition, until 1959. Today, located on the same site, the Pope Valley Winery is one of the most charming of the small wineries in these eastern mountains. Remaining are the blacksmith shop, a wagon shed, tools, and the original farmhouse. Among just four thousand cases of wine produced annually are a unique, dry Chenin Blanc, Cabernets, and other red wines, aged in a cellar that was hand-dug in 1909. Friends and wine lovers gather here in September at the Italian Harvest Party for a grape stomp and lots of pasta and wine; the Pope Valley Antique and Collectible Faire takes place on the grounds in October.

Drive far enough beyond Pope Valley to see hubcaps on trees, fences, and barns at Litto's Hubcap Ranch, where more than two thousand hubcabs were collected by Emanuele "Litto" Damonte, beginning in the 1930s. Litto's may be the only hubcap ranch in the world, and it is an official California Historic Landmark. Sparkling in the sun are more auto artifacts, too, from tires to hood ornaments. Litto died some years ago, at age eighty-nine, yet travelers continue to drop off spare hubcaps.

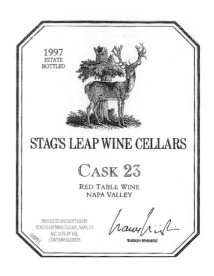

*Stag's Leap Wine Cellars produces three estate-grown Cabernets, including Cask 23, a blend of the best grapes from the winery's estate vineyards.*

**ABOVE:**
*Hot-air ballooning is a popular way to explore the wine country around Yountville and Oakville.*

**RIGHT:**
*The Chimney Rock Winery, located in the Stags Leap sub-appellation of the Napa Valley, reflects the glowing sunset.*

**FACING PAGE:**
*The Oakville Grocery is a gourmet food shop with old-time charm.*

## ROUTE 15

Explore the town of Yountville. Then, from the south end of Washington Street, take California Drive west, crossing beneath California Highway 29 to the Napa Valley Museum and Domaine Chandon. Take Washington Street north and go east on Yountville Cross Road to the Silverado Trail. Follow the Trail north, then take Oakville Cross Road west to Oakville at Highway 29.

### THE HOLLYWOOD CONNECTION

Just north of Yountville, one Napa Valley winery is linked to Hollywood. Niebaum-Coppola Estate Winery is owned by moviemaker Francis Ford Coppola, who restored one of the oldest winery estates in the valley, Inglenook, to its former glory. He drafted his set designers to create an extravaganza of a winery, featuring a gift store, museum, and park. A long allée of trees leads to the large Victorian-style park and its bubbling fountains, promenades, and lawns. You can walk through cool caves, where wine is stored behind iron bars, into high-ceilinged reception rooms resounding with Italian opera. Notice the gleaming exotic woods, the stained-glass windows, and an elaborate curving stairway leading to the museum. Ever see real Oscars up close? Here they are, Coppola's golden beauties, along with memorabilia from his life and his movies, including the boat from *Apocalypse Now* and costumes from *Bram Stoker's Dracula*.

Rainbow-hued hot-air balloons float, most early mornings, over the village of Yountville, where the few streets are lined with shade trees and cottages in overgrown country gardens. On the north end of town, a lovely cemetery is scattered with fascinating tombstones from the 1800s, including the grave of George Calvert Yount, founder of the town and the first white settler in the Napa Valley. Tombstones mark the resting places of Native Americans and early pioneers from New England, Canada, and Europe.

From the cemetery, you can take an easy, three-mile roundtrip walk or bike ride on Yount Mill Road, which runs along a tributary of the Napa River. Lined with big oaks, the deserted road is shady and bedecked with lovely views of the mountains and vineyards. Watch for a plaque honoring George Yount. In 1850s, he wangled from Spanish occupiers the huge land grant of Rancho Caymus, comprising much of the heart of the valley, and built grist- and sawmills on the river.

On the main drag of Yountville, Washington Street, stands Vintage 1870, a former winery within which a clutter of shops and cafés draws tourists. Also housing shops is the adjacent Southern Pacific Depot, where in the 1880s vacationers from San Francisco stopped off on their way north to the hot springs in Calistoga. Prior to the railroad, travelers came by steamboat up the Napa River and by stagecoach through the valley. Gordon's Café and Wine Bar in Yountville is the former stagecoach stop.

Another place to stroll is around the grounds of the old California Veterans Home, sited in a veritable botanical garden. A wide variety of trees was planted here in 1882 when the home, which is still in operation today, was built by veterans of the Mexican and Civil wars. Near the entrance to the home, the Napa Valley Museum showcases the culture and history of the valley and the art of winemaking.

Nearby the museum, Domaine Chandon is a sparkling-wine cellar where visitors sip bubbly while enjoying the elegant salon, lawns, and gardens. Whimsical art is on display throughout the property—look for a miniature forest of stone mushrooms under the oaks. Owned by Moët-Hennessy of France, Chandon was the first California sparkling-wine producer to be established by a French house and use only the traditional *méthode champenoise*.

French-inspired and French-owned restaurants are definitely in evidence in Yountville. Located in a vine-covered stone house, which was a saloon in 1900, the French Laundry has been praised as one of the best restaurants in the world; chef-owner Thomas Keller was named the top chef in America by the James Beard Foundation. Also holding forth are Bistro Jeanty, Bouchon, and the Restaurant at Domaine Chandon.

On Yountville Cross Road, a visit to Cliff Lede Vineyards offers the chance to see aging caves. The craggy pinnacles of Stags Leap on the eastern hills are the dramatic backdrop for the vineyards here in the Stags Leap viticultural area. Cabernet, Merlot, and a melony, lemony Brut sparkling wine are on the tasting menu. Deep in the caves, candlelight illuminates the cathedral ceilings and cobblestone floors.

Oakville Cross Road runs through the heart of the Cabernet Sauvignon vineyards of the Oakville viticultural area. Among several premium wineries here, Groth Vineyards and Winery attracts attention with its elaborate, rosy-pink, Spanish-Mission-style edifice surrounded by a hundred acres of Cabernet Sauvignon vineyards. In the public rooms, vivid, Expressionist-style paintings by Suzanne Groth depict the vineyard year.

Adjacent to the Groth estate, picnickers sit at tables overlooking the Cabernet vineyards at PlumpJack Winery, which was founded by San Francisco's forty-second mayor, Gavin Newsom. PlumpJack was the first premium winery to eschew traditional corks for screw cap closures, a move that other upscale producers have followed.

At Oakville Cross and California Highway 29, the Oakville Grocery, on the National Register of Historic Places, has been continuously operating since the late 1880s. The denizens of the village of Oakville in those days would have been astonished to find their grocery stocked with today's offerings of fresh foccacia and tapenade, hundreds of wines, artisan cheeses, olive oils, organic fruits, and French pastries.

## MOUNT VEEDER AND OAKVILLE GRADE
### A SHADY FOREST, ART, AND VALLEY VIEWS

Through a creek canyon and a forest of mossy oaks, fragrant bay trees, and tall redwoods and pines, Redwood Road and Mount Veeder Road twist and turn, ever narrowing, to reach isolated vineyards and wineries on the steep slopes of an extinct volcano, Mount Veeder. Deer, coyotes, foxes, and an occasional bobcat or black bear still roam in these wilds, where old orchards are vestiges of when the first white settlers lived here in the nineteenth century.

In the pure, cool mountain air, luxuriant herb and flower gardens flood the entry courtyard to the Hess Collection Winery on Redwood Road. Here an important display of European and American contemporary art resides in an enormous, ivy-covered, 1903 stone building. Among the works on view are those by major artists such as Francis Bacon, Frank Stella, and Robert Motherwell, all collected by Swiss-born winery founder, Donald Hess.

Situated near the summit of Mount Veeder, Mayacamas Winery was founded in 1889 by John Henry Fisher, a German immigrant and former pickle merchant. Fisher loaded his barrels of wine onto horse-drawn wagons and drove them fifteen miles down the mountain to the Napa River, where the

ROUTE 16

From California Highway 29 in Napa, take Redwood Road west to Hess Collection Winery. Backtrack on Redwood Road to Mount Veeder Road and take the latter northwest to Oakville Grade. Follow Oakville Grade east to Oakville at Highway 29.

*The Mediterranean-inspired winery at Groth Vineyards stands as a beacon through the early morning fog.*

**ABOVE:**
*Mount Veeder Road passes by vineyard after vineyard in the hills above the Napa Valley.*

**LEFT:**
*Sonoma County's Knights Valley, which runs along the border with Napa County, features quiet country lanes such as this.*

barrels were transported by ferry to San Francisco. At elevations between 1,800 and 2,400 feet, vines planted on steep, rocky slopes struggle through a growing season of summer heat spikes, abundant winter rain—as much as sixty inches in some years—and even occasional snowfalls, resulting in small crops of tiny Cabernet Sauvignon, Pinot Noir, and Chardonnay grapes.

At the north end of Mount Veeder Road, a mile-long, wooded road leads to Chateau Potelle, housed in a quaint, clapboard cottage framed by a majestic 360-degree view of mountains, valley, and vineyards. Although most of the Potelle wines are sold in retail shops, only here can you purchase their signature wines: Zinie de Potelle, a velvety, late-harvest, port-style wine, and Riviera, a dry, southern-French-style rosé made from a *saignee* of Syrah and Zinfandel. Under sunny skies, a glass of Riviera and a picnic lunch at Chateau Potelle can be an uplifting experience.

Toward the end of Oakville Grade, as it approaches California Highway 29, the curving lane of Acacia Drive is lined with a hundred gold-blooming gingko trees, heralding Far Niente Winery. The words *dolce far niente* are Italian for "the sweetness of doing nothing." The winery was founded in 1885 by John Benson, a Gold Rush–era entrepreneur and uncle of the American painter Winslow Homer. To design his monumental stone, gravity-fed winery, Benson hired his vineyard manager, a Scottish sea captain named Hamden McIntyre, who later became famous for creating the impressive Greystone, Trefethen, and Inglenook wineries. Owned today by the Nickel family, the three-story building is a jewel of dormered windows, thick, sandstone-block walls, arched vaults, and massive oak doors.

Guests at Far Niente are led through part of the forty-thousand-square-foot aging caves and into the Carriage House to see the classic automobiles and motorcycles collected by the late Gil Nickel, from a 1966 Ferrari 500 Superfast and a 1961 Corvette roadster to a one-off 1951 Ferrari 340 America. Samples of the award-winning Far Niente wines—Chardonnays, Oakville Cabernet Sauvignons, and Dolce, a sumptuous, late-harvest wine—are the final treats on the winery tour. Ask to see the oldest intact bottle of California wine in existence, a Far Niente Sweet Muscat, vintage 1886, enrobed in its original bottle and bearing its original cork and label.

## NAPA
## RING AROUND THE TOWN AND WOODEN VALLEY

The Napa River feeds into San Francisco Bay, which made the town of Napa an important staging site for the shipment of goods during the Gold Rush of the 1850s. On the west side of the river in Napa, Victorian-era neighborhoods remain, restored to their brightly painted, rococo glory. A red and green trolley trundles along the revitalized Riverfront District to historic buildings transformed into retail and restaurant complexes. As fancy as a decorated wedding cake, the 1879 Napa Opera House is now the venue for concerts, drama, and cabaret. Where steamships once picked up cargo from the wharf at the cavernous Hatt Warehouse, waterfront cafés, a luxury hotel, a wine bar, and an outdoor stage are among the attractions.

ROUTE 17

From downtown Napa, take California Highway 29 north to Trancas Street; take Trancas east to Big Ranch Road. Take Big Ranch Road north, Oak Knoll Avenue east, and the Silverado Trail south. Go east on Hardiman Avenue to Atlas Peak Road; follow Atlas Peak Road north to Del Dotto Caves and Hedgeside Wine Gallery, then reverse direction and head south to Monticello Road. Go east on Monticello to Wooden Valley Road, and follow Wooden Valley Road east and south to Altamura Vineyards and Winery. Return to Napa by way of Monticello Road, or continue south on Wooden Valley Road and Suisun Valley Road to Interstate 80.

East of town, the low foothills of the eastern Vaca Range begin to rise, topped by Atlas Peak at 2,660 feet. On Big Ranch Road, the knolls of the Oak Knoll viticultural area collect the chill air and afternoon breezes that blow in from San Pablo Bay, resulting in cooler temperatures than up the valley and making this AVA one of the rare places warm enough to ripen Cabernet Sauvignon and Merlot grapes, without being too warm for Chardonnay and Pinot Noir.

Around a Tuscan-style piazza, the Andretti Winery is the brainchild of race car legend Mario Andretti, who is sometimes on hand to greet visitors and talk about his days on the Daytona and Indianapolis raceways. Available only at the winery are Andretti wines under the Montona label, named for Mario's birthplace in Northern Italy.

A handful of wineries on Big Ranch Road are architecturally interesting. At Monticello Vineyards, the pink-brick Jefferson House is a delightful, quarter-sized version of Thomas Jefferson's famous Monticello home in Virginia.

On the north side of Oak Knoll Avenue, one of the winding lanes crossing the valley, Trefethen Vineyards is the only surviving example of what was once the most common winery architecture in Napa, a three-story, wooden, gravity-flow winery. A historic landmark, the winery was designed and built by Hamden McIntyre.

On the Silverado Trail, you may think you have taken a wrong turn when you see a forest of eighteen-foot-tall, freestanding, golden columns topped with capital bulls. These columns mark the entrance to Darioush, one of the most unusual wineries in the state, if not the country. Inspired by the architecture of Persepolis, the ancient capital of Persia, the Darioush family erected a temple to Persian culture and premium Napa Valley wine. Pale, gold travertine blocks from the Middle East clad the visitor's center, where waving palms, formal Mediterranean gardens, and indoor and outdoor water features create a setting fit for royalty. In the sleek tasting room, guests wander the polished floors among carved columns, sipping Bordeaux varietals such as Viognier, Shiraz, and a luscious late-harvest Sauvignon Blanc.

A vine-draped, stone-walled wine gallery and caves await the oenophile at Del Dotto Vineyards, Caves and Wine Gallery on Atlas Peak Road. In the ivy-covered, marble-floored 1884 Hedgeside Distillery Building and in hand-dug limestone caves from the same era, the winery offers an in-depth introduction to winemaking. A wine "thief," a device used to take samples from barrels of wine, draws out samples of wines aged in a Missouri oak barrel, a Virginia oak barrel, a Troncais French oak barrel, and a Nevers French oak barrel, for visitors to taste the difference.

Oak, manzanita, and bay trees hang over Monticello Road, where stone ramparts hint at the rocky conditions in which the legendary Cabernets of Jarvis Winery are grown. Tunneled into a mountainside, forty-five thousand square feet of caves shelter the entire winemaking facility at Jarvis; the last chamber of the caves could comfortably contain a basketball court. Along with a running stream and a waterfall, glowing wall sconces, arched alcoves, and fiber-optic chandeliers create a romantic atmosphere. The creator of the wines is Dimitri Tchelistcheff, son of one of the fathers of the California wine industry, André Tchelistcheff.

**RIGHT:**
**RIGHT:**
*Modernist fountains and sculptures distinguish the Artesa Vineyards and Winery in Los Carneros.*

**BELOW:**
*The sunrise light illuminates the wine barrels at Bouchaine Vineyards, the oldest winery in the Carneros region of Napa County.*

**RIGHT:**
*Located less than three miles from Artesa Winery—but architecturally a world away—Domaine Carneros is a leading producer of California sparkling wines.*

**FACING PAGE:**
*Grape vines and mustard plants stretch into the horizon in early spring in the lower Carneros region. San Francisco Bay is visible in the distance.*

Not in the least bit of danger from vehicle traffic, wild turkeys prattle across Wooden Valley Road. Nearly a thousand feet higher in elevation than the floor of the Napa Valley, Wooden Valley is also several degrees cooler most days and nights, a perfect climate for growing Cabernet Sauvignon and Sangiovese grapes on the hillsides around Altamura Vineyards and Winery.

Frank and Karen Altamura's family has owned a four-hundred-acre patch of Wooden Valley since 1855. Guarding the entrance to the winery, mossy old oaks and gigantic boulders are craggy backdrops for the rows of vines sweeping up into low hills. In the cool aging caves, the nose of the wine is of dried violets and lavender and the taste is of dark chocolate, currant, and perhaps raspberry, with a cocoa finish. The Altamura Sangioveses have been compared to the legendary Brunellos of Montalcino, in Italy; and in fact, the Altamura rootstock was grafted with Brunello clones.

Beyond Altamura, going south, Wooden Valley Road becomes Suisun Valley Road, where a handful of wineries lie in the bucolic Suisun Valley viticultural area.

## LOS CARNEROS
### TOP OF THE BAY

ROUTE 18

From California Highway 29 at California Highway 12/121, take 12/121 west to Old Sonoma Road, driving a short distance east to Dealy Lane, which runs north to Henry Road. After exploring the area, return to Highway 12/121 and cross it to reach Duhig Road. Drive south on Duhig, east on Las Amigas Road, and south on Buchli Station Road. Back on Las Amigas, go east to Cuttings Wharf Road, north to Highway 12/121, and a short distance west to the di Rosa Preserve.

America's largest private collection of contemporary art, sparkling wine with French and Spanish connections, and a winery that disappears into the hills are some of the pleasures of Los Carneros, a grape-growing district on the southern borders of both Napa and Sonoma counties. A few old farmhouses recall the days when sheep and dairy cows grazed the hills and hay was the main crop, before these lowlands were discovered to be prime real estate for growing Pinot Noir and Chardonnay.

Three miles from the north end of San Pablo Bay, which connects with the dependably chilly San Francisco Bay, the Carneros viticultural area is known for a unique lowland *terroir* comprising shallow, rocky clay soil and cool ocean breezes. The growing season is long, rainfall is minimal, and the yields per vine are low, resulting in grapes of concentrated fruit character and high acidity, increasing the wines' ability to age.

West of Napa on Henry Road, and not easily noticed, Artesa Vineyards is a modernist-style winery built right into a hillside and covered over with lush native grasses. Visitors ascend past waterfalls and reflecting pools to a patio with a dazzling view of the Carneros and Napa valleys. The reception area is at once an art gallery and a wine museum, where artist-in-residence Gordon Huether has installed a striking array of glass and metal sculptures. Owned by Codorníu, Spain's largest producer of sparking wine, Artesa makes Cabernet Sauvignon, Pinot Noir, Chardonnay, and a unique Spanish varietal, Tempranillo.

In stark contrast to the architectural and artistic panache of Artesa, Carneros Creek Winery, just down the road, is a small, friendly place with picnic tables under a vine-covered arbor. Among honors accorded to their Pinot Noir is the official designation as the wine of Cork, the Irish city where the winery owner, Francis Mahoney, was born.

On Duhig Road at California Highway 12/121, fleecy willow trees and Chardonnay and Pinot Noir vineyards surround the grand double staircase leading to the Louis XV–style salon at Domaine Carneros, where a portrait of Madame de Pompadour awaits the arrival of guests. Built by the French house of Taittinger, this majestic winery was modeled after the eighteenth-century chateau owned by the Taittinger family in Champagne, France. The terrace is a pleasant perch from which to overlook the hills and vineyards of Carneros while sipping sparkling wines redolent of citrus, melon, nutty spice, and even roses. The winery also produces classic Carneros Pinot Noirs and Chardonnays.

One of the leaders of modern winemaking in the Carneros in the late 1970s, Acacia Vineyard, on Las Amigas Road, manages to produce Pinots that are darker, richer, and more fragrant than those typically associated with this cool appellation. Some of their full-bodied Chardonnays have been described as tasting of fig, butter, apple, and hazelnut. The picnic lawn under the olive trees at Acacia offers big views of the district, south to the top of the bay.

On Buchli Station Road, the design of renowned architect William Turnbull distinguishes Bouchaine Vineyards, which is the oldest continually operating winery in the Carneros. The property was planted with vines and fruit trees in the mid-1800s by a man named Boon Fly and later by the Garetto brothers, who made grappa, whiskey, and sacramental wines. Reclaimed redwood wine tanks were used for siding the Bouchaine winery, wherein a cozy reception area welcomes visitors to linger by the fireplace and look out into the rolling hills.

At the end of Buchli Station Road is a forty-thousand-acre area known as the Napa-Sonoma Marshes Wildlife Area, where well over a hundred species of birds and waterfowl are permanent residents or seasonal migrants in the salt marshes and ponds and in the freshwater wetlands. Notable are the endangered California clapper rail and three threatened species: the California black rail, the salt marsh yellow throat, and the western snowy plover. A roofed wildlife-viewing blind overlooking a reedy pond and a popular feeding area is open to the public. Binoculars will help you see many colorful birds, from graceful egrets and great blue herons to coots, canvasbacks, and red-winged blackbirds. The rusty-brown-backed ruddy duck has a distinctive, bright-blue beak. Napa County has one of the largest diversifications of bird life of any county in the United States.

Surrounded by another nature preserve, the di Rosa Preserve consists of rambling galleries housed in modern versions of farm buildings and in a nineteenth century manor house. On exhibit are a huge and rather startling collection of California Bay Area contemporary art. You will see cars hanging in trees, a sixty-five-foot-tall stack of file cabinets, hundreds of paintings, trumpeting peacocks, and grazing cows and sheep—some of them art, some living and breathing. All of this art exists in an idyllic countryside environment of vineyards and olive trees, a lake, meadows, and palm trees.

*Bouchaine's main building, updated by architect William Turnbull in 1995, adorns the label of the winery's fine Pinots.*

# PART IV

# SIERRA FOOTHILLS:
# VINTAGE GOLD COUNTRY

**FACING PAGE:**
*The Old West mystique is alive and well in the foothills of California's Sierra Nevada, as evident in this field near Murphys.*

**ABOVE:**
*A sign lets you know what lies ahead on this dusty road in Calaveras County. The winery up here is Twisted Oak.*

The Sierra Foothills viticultural area is a warm, dry region stretching through the western foothills of the massive wall of the Sierra Nevada mountain range. In the mid-1800s, gold was discovered along the corridors of the six major rivers that plunge out of the Sierra: the Yuba, the American, the Mokelumne, the Stanislaus, the Tuolumne, and the Merced. For a decade or so after the 1848 discovery of gold, boomtowns exploded in population, only to be abandoned when the lodes were exhausted just a few years later. Hell-bent on striking it rich, immigrant miners and gold panners, predominantly European, brought with them Old World grapevine cuttings, primarily Zinfandel. By the 1870s, there were a hundred wineries in the Gold Country. Some of the original Zinfandel vines are still producing.

After Prohibition, the wine industry faded until the 1970s, when winemaking throughout the state began an upswing. The climate and soil conditions in the foothills, which vary dramatically according to elevation, are ideal for Zinfandel, Syrah, and Sauvignon Blanc, and on the cooler slopes of El Dorado County, they are perfect for Rhône varietals.

For wine lovers who are also history buffs and outdoor enthusiasts, little-known premium wineries are to be discovered here, along with many Gold Rush museums, ruins, and historic sites; picturesque Western towns; and recreation such as hiking, biking, camping, and water sports. Nearly all of the wineries were established in the last quarter of the twentieth century; most are small and located on scenic country roads.

The sleepy, nineteenth-century small towns that remain today are loaded with Old West artifacts, antiques, and whimsical architecture, from gingerbread-bedecked Victorian hotels to cowboy saloons, false-front general stores, and miners' cabins turned into quaint cottages. A completely restored small town, now a state park, Columbia re-creates the daily life and the resident population of an authentic Gold Rush–era town.

## EL DORADO COUNTY
### FAIR PLAY GETAWAY

ROUTE 19

From Placerville, take Diamond Road south to Diamond Springs. Follow Pleasant Valley Road east and take a sidetrip west on Leisure Lane at Pleasant Valley. Return to Pleasant Valley Road, then follow Mount Aukum Road south to Mount Aukum.

Take Omo Ranch Road east and Fair Play Road north, from which you can drive east onto Slug Gulch Road and Oakstone Winery. Return to Fair Play Road, then head west on Perry Creek Road to reconnect with Mount Aukum Road.

Enjoying a cooler climate than elsewhere in the Sierra foothills, vineyards in El Dorado County are planted between 1,200 and 3,600 feet in elevation, where low daytime temperatures, more rain, and less topsoil create a *terroir* amenable to the growing of Bordeaux grape varieties such as Cabernet Sauvignon, Merlot, and Cabernet Franc. In a few warm pockets, the traditional foothills wine grape, Zinfandel, soaks up the heat.

Within the El Dorado and Fair Play viticultural areas, nearly two dozen mostly family-owned wineries can be found on a network of country roads east and southeast of Placerville. Holly's Hill Vineyards, on a ridge above Leisure Lane in the El Dorado appellation, is a perfect vantage point from which to view spectacular snowcapped mountains framing the Cosumnes River Canyon. In rocky soil on steep, terraced slopes, the vineyards are planted with Rhône varietals: Syrah, Grenache, Mourvedre, Roussanne, and Viognier. Along with neighbors Sierra Vista and Narrow Gate Vineyards,

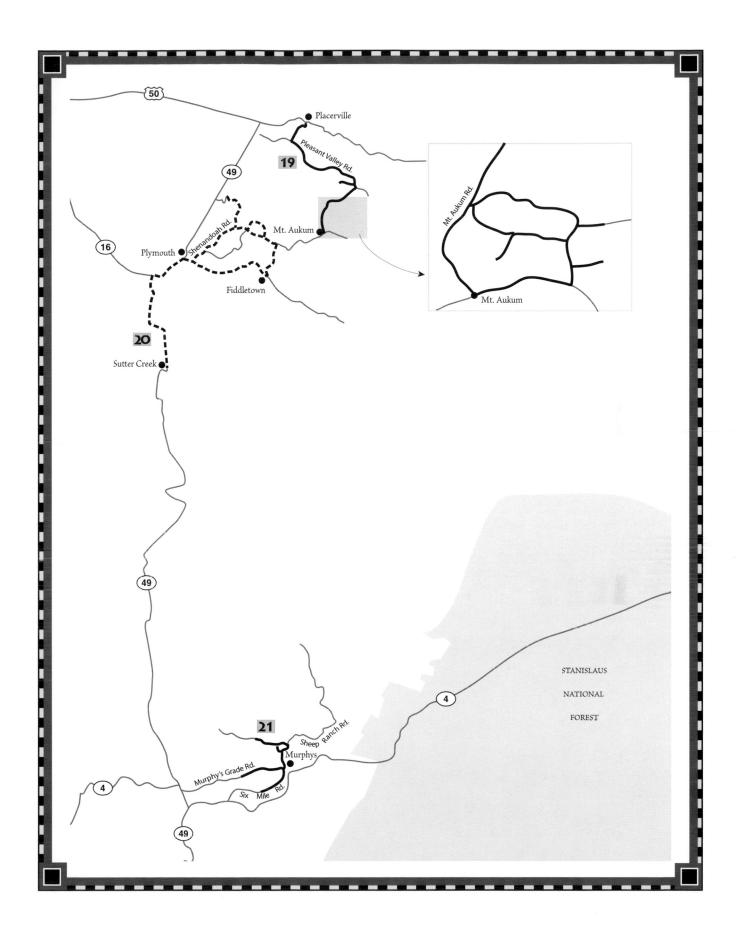

50

Placerville

19

Pleasant Valley Rd.

49

Shenandoah Rd.

Mt. Aukum Rd.

Mt. Aukum

16

Plymouth

Shenandoah Rd.

Mt. Aukum

Fiddletown

20

Sutter Creek

STANISLAUS

NATIONAL

FOREST

49

4

21

Sheep Ranch Rd.

Murphys

Murphy's Grade Rd.

Six Mile Rd.

4

49

**RIGHT:**
*An old wine press sits outside the historic Lombardo home-stead at the Boeger Winery near Placerville.*

**BELOW:**
*A creative pumpkin display celebrates the fall harvest at an apple orchard in El Dorado County.*

**Clockwise from top:**

*The deck at the Fitzpatrick Winery and Lodge offers sweeping views of the surrounding countryside.*

*After sampling Fitzpatrick's organic wines, you can relax by the pool at the lodge in the scenic Sierra foothills of El Dorado County.*

*A bust of Dionysus, the Greek god of wine, is on display in the Great Room at the Fitzpatrick Winery and Lodge.*

Holly's Hill is a member of "El DôRhone," an exclusive consortium of county wineries known for producing Rhône-style wines.

The tiny appellation of Fair Play, granted the status of an American Viticultural Area in 1980, comprises less than a dozen small wineries in a triangle of roads between the historic little communities of Mount Aukum, Fair Play, and Somerset. On a hilltop above Fairplay Road, the deck at Fitzpatrick Winery affords a wide view of the AVA. As the wine grapes here are grown organically, cover crops of native wildflowers fill the vineyard rows. Within a massive log lodge is a winery, downstairs, and a small inn, upstairs. Entranced by the dream of participating in a harvest, some guests settle in for what is called "A Crushing Experience," when everyone gets into overalls and lends a hand with the picking, followed by a hands-on, in-depth introduction to de-stemming, crushing, fermenting, blending, and barrel tasting—all in all, a rare opportunity for wine aficionados.

True to their Irish heritage, the Fitzpatricks put on an all-day St. Patrick's Day celebration, complete with homemade Guinness Beef Stew, bread baked in wood-fired ovens, Celtic Cider, and wine, including an unusual blend called Tir Na Nog, which is a robust combination of Nebbiolo, Sangiovese, and Zinfandel grapes.

Not to be outdone, Oakstone Winery on Slug Gulch Road lays out samples of Zinfandel, Sangiovese, and its premium estate-bottled Bordeaux-style blends. When you turn onto Slug Gulch Road, cross the little bridge at the battalion of mailboxes and go up the hill past Boondock Trail. You will know you are in the right place when you see the sign that reads, "Wine Tasting 564 feet."

In addition to their premium estate wines, Oakstone has made itself famous with its notorious Slug Gulch Red table wine. Legend has it that during one of the annual countywide wine festivals, a busload of raucous oenophiles who had heard tell of the zesty and quite affordable red careened up the steep hill to the winery and leaned out the windows of the bus chanting, "Slug Gulch! Slug Gulch!" That particular vintage sold out before the

## APPLE HILL

East of Placerville, a web of curvy roads called Apple Hill makes for a pretty drive any time of year. From early fall through the end of the year, the country lanes are thronged with foliage peepers and fruit lovers visiting more than fifty ranches and farms, a handful of wineries, and roadside stands and stores selling pies, juices, jams, dried fruits, and nuts.

Abel's Apple Acres on Carson Road offers buttermilk apple pie, cider, and apple butter. Drive off Carson and onto Larsen Road at Larsen's Ranch and ask to see the Rhode Island Greening, believed to be the oldest ap-

ple tree in the county. Apple dumplings are on the menu at Grandpa's Cellar, nestled under the pines and incense cedars on Cable Road. A short, signed nature trail leads to two neighboring ranches, notably Bolster's Hilltop Ranch, where heirloom apples are the specialty.

Boeger Winery on Carson Road, one of the wineries in the Apple Hill district, offers samples of their Hangtown Red and the Italian varietals Nebbiolo and Barbera. Visitors picnic in the pear orchard or redwood grove by the pond and take photos of the antique car and truck collection.

festival was over. At the California State Fair, Slug Gulch Red, a blend of Syrah, Carignane, and Sangiovese grapes, won "Best Red Table Wine with a California Appellation."

Perched on another breezy hilltop, on Perry Creek Road above the middle fork of the Cosumnes River, Perry Creek Vineyards is the home of the award-winning Zin Man Zinfandel, a zesty concoction with aromas of raspberry and cherry and hints of spice and oak. Visitors gather on the wisteria-draped veranda to picnic and sip wine. In the winery's elegant, Mission-style tasting room, African baskets and fair-trade handcrafts from Latin America are for sale.

## SHENANDOAH VALLEY
### GOLD RUSH TOWN, ITALIAN WINES

Amador County is rolling pastures, vineyards, and orchard lands, criss-crossed by rivers that produced more gold than any other county in the Mother Lode. In the mid-1800s, $300 million in gold was mined along the Mokelumne River, alone.

Several still-alive-and-kicking Gold Rush–era towns and many abandoned settlements look much as they did in the nineteenth century. The picturesque towns of Sutter Creek, Plymouth, and Fiddletown are where travelers rest, eat, and shop between excursions on the backroads.

Cradled in oak-dotted hills, the white frame houses of Sutter Creek give the town a New England look. On and around Main Street is a rich cache of vintage architecture, including elaborately painted Victorians, Western false-fronts with overhanging balconies, and even a Greek Revival church—United Methodist, a circa-1860 beauty with tall steeples. A tribute to the 1940s, the Chatter Box Café is an old-fashioned soda fountain complete with World War II posters and Big Band records. Winemakers and farmers meet at the long counter for burgers, pie, and ice cream sodas.

Knight's Foundry, on Eureka Street, is the only water-powered foundry still operating in the United States. Beginning in 1873, the foundry produced just about every forged or cast piece of machinery called for by industries throughout this part of the state. From water wheels to ornamental Victorian iron gates to gold-mining equipment, all of it was made here. Today, the foundry is a National Historic Site and is open for tours by arrangement.

North of Sutter Creek, about two dozen wineries are located in old barns and stone cellars on side roads that branch off Shenandoah Road. Vineyards thrive in long, hot growing seasons and cold, dry winters. Planted in soils of decomposed granite and of iron-laden, brick-red dirt similar to that found in Tuscany, Mediterranean varietals are making the county famous for Zinfandel, Barbera, and Sangiovese. Some of the spicy, hearty, old-vine Zinfandels come from vines planted in the 1860s.

In operation since 1856, when it was founded by a Swiss family, Sobon Estate and Shenandoah Vineyards is the oldest winery in the region. In the charming Shenandoah Valley Museum on the grounds are huge, old wine

ROUTE 20

Explore Sutter Creek, then drive north on California Highway 49 and east on California Highway 16 to Plymouth. Follow Shenandoah Road east to Ostrom Road, making detours on Bell Road and Steiner Road along the way. Head south on Ostrom Road to Fiddletown and west on Fiddletown Road back to Plymouth.

*This mid-nineteenth-century lithograph shows a comical gold prospector making his way to California, loaded down with tools and supplies.*

*Shenandoah Vineyards is located among the rolling hillsides of Amador County.*

*Steve's Antiques on Fiddletown Road captures the feel of Gold Rush–era California.*

*The Sobon Estates vineyard, originally planted in 1856, is the oldest vineyard in the region and one of the oldest in the entire state.*

casks and displays of antique farming, winemaking, and household implements. Shirley and Leon Sobon and some of their six children organically grow Cal-Ital varietals, and they pioneered the planting of French Rhône varietals in these foothills.

Specializing in the Italian varietal Sangiovese, made in the Chianti Classico style, Vino Noceto welcomes visitors to its 1887 ranch house amid a grove of nearly a hundred walnut trees. Summertime is the season to enjoy the lively Moscato Bianco called Frivolo, an effervescent Muscat blend, and the rosé-style Rosato Sangiovese, a perfect picnic wine. Braver souls enjoy a nip or two of the Grappa di Sangiovese. To herald the beginning of the growing season, the winery invites all to come in April for bluegrass music, bocce ball, food, and wine.

North of Shenandoah Road on Bell Road, in a nineteenth-century bunkhouse pocked with woodpecker holes, oenophiles line up at secluded Story Winery for Zinfandel and Mission wines produced from some of the oldest vines in the state. Barrel tastings of vintages not yet ready for bottling are available most weekends.

By far the largest and most modern of the Amador County wineries, Montevina Winery produces the most diverse array of Italian varietals in California. Under a vine-draped arbor, you can sip, and try to pronounce, little-known wines such as Aglianico, Teroldego, Freisa, and Refosco.

A barrel maker from Indiana, John J. Davis arrived in the area in 1852 and shortly thereafter found eighty-five ounces of gold in one week. Around 1853, he planted Mission grapevines, and later, his son planted Zinfandel vines; both vineyards are still producing at Deaver Wineyards. Following his grandfather Davis' lead, Ken Deaver continues to make velvety Zinfandel, in addition to classic Sangiovese and Barbera and rich ports. Old barns and an oak-framed lake setting make this winery a nice stop on Steiner Road.

## Calaveras County
### Murphys, Caverns, and Big Reds

ROUTE 21

From Murphys, take sidetrips west on Six Mile Road and Murphy's Grade Road. Then from Murphys, drive north on Sheep Ranch Road.

Bullet holes in the front door of the Murphys Hotel are reminders of the good old days of the late 1870s when the notorious stagecoach-robbing highwayman, Black Bart, trod the wooden sidewalks of the town of Murphys. Ulysses S. Grant and Mark Twain each sat a spell on the hotel veranda, before the locust trees became the tall umbrellas they are today.

Known as Murphys Rich Diggins when the Wells Fargo office shipped out $15.4 million in gold from local placer mines, Murphys declined into obscurity after the Gold Rush. Fortunately for today's residents and visitors, the town escaped the twentieth-century remodeling that occurred in many Mother Lode towns, and as a result, much of the original architecture remains on Main Street, which runs along burbling Murphys Creek. You can hang out right in Murphys, where several wineries have tasting rooms, or you can take a horse-drawn wagon tour around town and on scenic backroads to nearby wineries.

Located in an old carriage house and former Flying A gas station, Milliaire Winery is a popular gathering place at harvest time, when crushing and pressing take place in view of passersby. Milliaire makes traditional Gewürztraminer and Chardonnay, a unique Orange Muscat, a "Simply Red" table wine, and a Zinfandel port.

On Algiers Street, the Malvadino Vineyards tasting room offers a chance to try wines made from Mission grapes grown on vines well over a century old. The Spanish *padres* who established mission churches in California in the 1700s were the first to plant this varietal, with which they made sacramental wines. They stored their wine in hide pouches; Malvadino wines are aged in French oak, making them, likely, much more drinkable.

On Main Street and also at a winery on Red Hill Road near Vallecito, Twisted Oak Winery offers samples of its whimsically named wines. A piquant red, "The Spaniard" is a unique Tempranillo, Cabernet Sauvignon, and Petit Verdot blend; while "Murgatroyd" is an age-worthy, Bordeaux-style marriage of Cabernet Sauvignon and Petite Verdot.

At Black Sheep Vintners on Main Street and Murphy's Grade Road, a 1920s barn with a rusting metal roof houses the winery where Jan and Dave Olson make voluptuous, spicy Zinfandels, the most prominent varietal grown in the region. A smooth Cabernet Franc is dense with berry flavors, while the hearty table wine, True Frogs Lily Pad Red, blends Zinfandel and Cinsault.

The harvest is celebrated each year in October at the Calaveras Grape Stomp and Murphys Gold Rush Street Faire, highlighted by a raucous grape-stomping competition. Dressed in period clothes or in crazy costumes of their choice, stompers climb into wooden barrels and smash twenty-five pounds of grapes at a time, while their "swappers" lean in to keep the drain clear of stems and seeds. After several rounds, sticky, drippy, and red from head to toe, the competitors repair to the massage tent, while spectators browse the Street Faire and indulge in barbecue, wine tasting, face painting, belly dancing, and general kicking up of heels.

Surrounding Murphys, in a rolling landscape of grassy, oak- and pine-dotted hills, are a handful of wineries that sprouted up in the 1980s and 1990s. Just a mile out of town on Six Mile Road, Ironstone Vineyards presents a multifaceted experience for wine, garden, and history lovers. In the seven-story main building, visitors congregate by the forty-foot-tall limestone fireplace, enjoying a collection of Western art and majestic sounds from the 1927 movie-theater pipe organ. In the Heritage Museum are specimens of locally discovered gold, including the largest crystalline gold-leaf nugget in the world, a forty-four pounder. Wine tasters explore hand-dug aging caverns and belly up to a 1907 rococo bar, while flower fanciers wander the cattail-lined shores of a small lake, herb gardens, and colorful banks of rhododendrons, azaleas, and camellias. Thousands of daffodils and other bulbs burst into bloom in the spring, a cause for celebration at the annual Spring Obsession festival of wine, food, art, and flowers.

Gerber Vineyards on Six Mile Road holds forth in a perfectly restored 1800s farmhouse surrounded by white picket fences. An Emmy-winning,

*The rustic winery building at the Black Sheep Winery is adorned with lush vines and other plantings.*

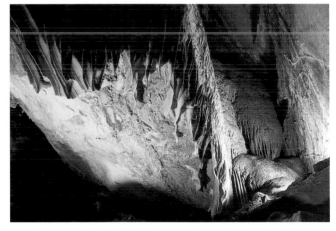

**CLOCKWISE FROM TOP:**
*Getting around the hilly vineyards at the Stevenot Winery is best accomplished on four wheels.*

*John Mercer came upon this three-million-year-old cave while searching for gold in 1885. Today Mercer Caverns is a popular tourist attraction in the Sierra foothills.*

*A worker "punches down" wine in a fermentation tank at the Twisted Oak Winery. This technique is used to ensure maximum extraction from the cap of grape skins that forms as the wine ferments.*

*Massive metal tanks stand alongside traditional oak barrels in the breezeway outside Ironstone Vineyards' wine caverns.*

former Hollywood and television movie producer, David Gerber, and his actress wife, Laraine Stephens, operate the largest vineyard in Calaveras County. Under the Laraine label, they make Chardonnay, Merlot, and Syrah.

An old wagon road, Sheep Ranch Road winds out of Murphys to Mercer Caverns. No trip to the Sierra foothills is complete without a tour of one of four natural wonders: the underground caverns of Mercer Caverns, Black Chasm, Moaning Cavern, or California Cavern. Not as fearsome as they sound, each cavern consists of huge chambers connected by well-lighted walkways, platforms, and stairs designed to give breathtaking views of vividly colored limestone chambers spiked with stalactite and stalagmite formations. The atmosphere is delightfully spooky and damp, and with a constant temperature in the high fifties, the caverns are refreshing in summer when outside it may be more than a hundred degrees in the shade.

Off Sheep Ranch Road on San Domingo Road, in a wooded valley at 1,900 feet in elevation, Stevenot Winery offers samples of its medal-winning Zinfandel, Chardonnay, and Cabernet Sauvignon in a sod-roofed former miner's cabin. In the summertime, the Murphys Creek Theatre presents Shakespearean plays outdoors in the winery's amphitheater.

In the most perfectly re-created Mother Lode settlement in the United States, Columbia State Historic Park, costumed townspeople rumble along the dirt streets in horse-drawn wagons and surreys. Storekeepers, smudge-faced blacksmiths, street musicians, candle makers, and innkeepers contribute to the living-history atmosphere.

When gold was discovered in California in 1848, the town of Columbia grew within a month from a population of less than a hundred to more than six thousand people, and 150 saloons, gambling halls, hostelries, and stores opened up. Many of the Western false-front and brick buildings with iron shutters remain, housing the shops, restaurants, and museums of today.

Horse-drawn stages clip-clop up and down the street. Artisans demonstrate horseshoeing, woodcarving, and other vintage crafts. You can pan for gold in the nearby creeks, take a horseback ride, and have a sarsaparilla at the old-fashioned ice cream parlor. The firemen regularly haul out their gold- and red-painted hand-pumper, the Papeete, built in Boston in 1852.

Among a lively schedule of annual events in Columbia are the colorful Fireman's Muster in May and the Fiddle and Banjo Contest in October.

*The town of Columbia sprang up in 1850 in the heart of the Mother Lode during the great California Gold Rush.*

# PART V

# CENTRAL COAST AND VALLEYS: SEA BREEZES, MOUNTAIN MISTS

**FACING PAGE:**
*Coastal mist creeps through hills above the Carmel Valley in Monterey County.*

**ABOVE:**
*Pelicans gather on the rocks at Natural Bridges Beach State Park on the Santa Cruz coast.*

Viticultural areas in California's central valleys and coast regions are relatively new developments in the history of winemaking. Unlike other wine regions in the state that are largely carpeted in vineyards, here vast fields of vegetable crops, historic cattle and horse ranches, and pure mountain wilderness dominate the landscape.

A few miles inland from Monterey Bay and reaching southeast for about seventy miles, Monterey County is teased with foggy fingers and cool sea breezes that creep into narrow inland valleys from the nearby Pacific Ocean. Mists collect on the shoulders of the Santa Lucia Mountains. These mountains shelter the golden, pastoral Carmel Valley, where cowboys and dudes ride the range and a handful of wineries produce Bordeaux-style wines.

Santa Lucia Highlands is a new and growing viticultural area sharing the Salinas Valley with lettuce and strawberry fields. Giant-sized painted figures of farm workers along the roadside and a museum dedicated to an American literary light are found in this pastoral valley.

Drenching winter rains and occasional snow create challenging *terroirs* in the Santa Cruz Mountains appellation, where slow drives on a twisting labyrinth of backroads lead to ancient redwood forests and sunny riverbanks. Lovers of Rhône-style wines make their pilgrimages to the widely scattered, small wineries here, seeking the intense, complicated flavors and distinctive character found only in these mountain-grown wines.

In San Benito County's remote Cienega Valley, beyond the quiet, shady streets of a California mission town, are wineries and winemakers of singular character.

## THE SANTA CRUZ MOUNTAINS
### REDWOODS AND WINE

ROUTE 22

From California Highway 17 just south of Los Gatos, take Bear Creek Road west to Boulder Creek. Follow California Highway 236 north to Big Basin Redwoods State Park; reverse direction and return on Highway 236 to Boulder Creek. Head south on California Highway 9 to Felton and take Felton Empire Road west, Empire Grade north, and Pine Flat Road south. Loop back to Felton by following Martin Road, Ice Cream Grade, and Felton Empire Road east. Return to Highway 17 by going south on Graham Hill Road.

In the misty aerie of the Santa Cruz Mountains are dappled redwood groves and aromatic fir forests, sunny riverbanks, quiet little resort towns, covered bridges, and a rollicking steam train. There are wineries, too, here in the highest, coolest California viticultural area.

Far above the hazy, sometimes too hot Silicon Valley and the beaches of Santa Cruz, the rugged mountain slopes are cooled by marine fogs nearly every night and menaced by strong winter storms, and the soils are stony and thin, producing low crop levels and concentrated grape flavors. This singular *terroir* favors Rhône varietals and Chardonnay grapes, and in a few sunny pockets, Merlot, Cabernet Sauvignon, and Zinfandel. As it was the first wine-growing region in the nation to be defined by a mountain range, the appellation is called "America's Premier Mountain Appellation," and comprises about fifty small wineries.

A corkscrew route, Bear Creek Road, leads to Byington Winery, which stands at an elevation of two thousand feet. Byington's palatial Italianate stone chateau is an elegant milieu for the introduction of their vineyard-designated

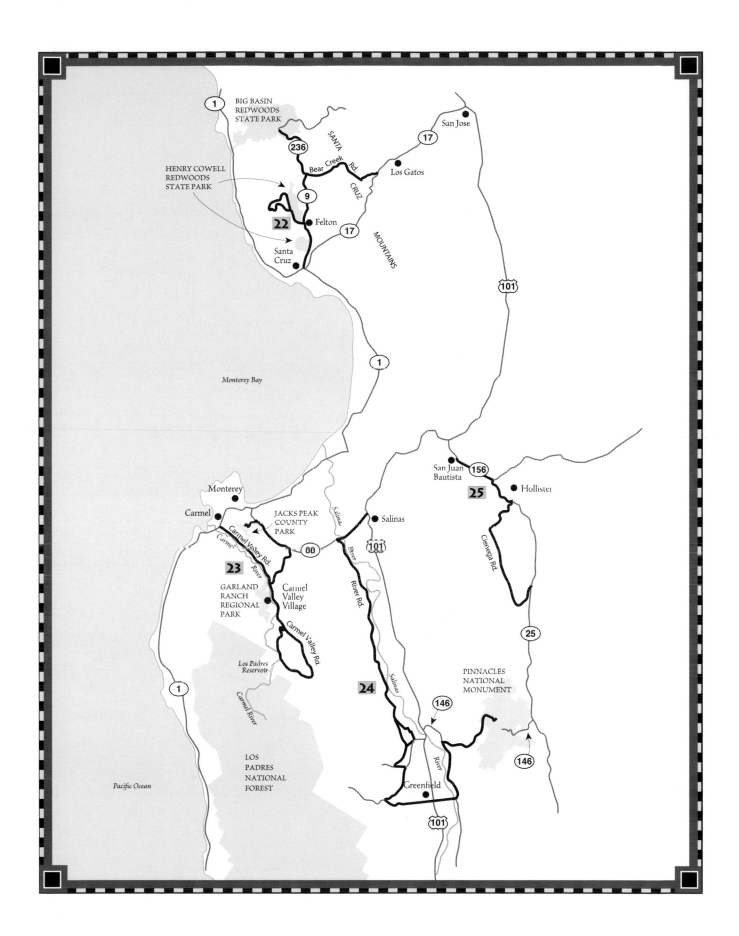

**THIS PAGE:**
*Fambrini's Farm Fresh Produce grows and distributes organic fruits and vegetables from its farmlands near Davenport, on Highway 1 north of Santa Cruz.*

**FACING PAGE:**
*Ponderosa pines and manzanita grow in the sand hills of the Bonny Doon Ecological Reserve, managed by the California Department of Fish and Game.*

Chardonnays and Bordeaux-style wines. The Cabernet Sauvignon is grown on steep hillsides on the southern slopes of Mount Madonna in the south end of the appellation.

Across the road in a minimalist reception hall, David Bruce Winery has for more than four decades been renowned for gold-medal-winning Pinot Noir and Chardonnay.

In the one-horse town of Boulder Creek, quaint cottages and picket fences, chain saw sculptures, whimsical redwood burl furniture, and antique stores are among the attractions. The 1860s was a rollicking time in this logging town of saloons, gambling houses, and brothels. Some late-nineteenth-century architecture remains on the main street, housing art galleries and cafés.

Big Basin Redwoods State Park can be accessed from Boulder Creek by California Highway 236. Here, in the oldest of California's state parks, thousand-year-old redwoods stand like druids of old. Waterfalls, stream canyons, huckleberry bushes, and mushrooms are highlights on nearly a hundred miles of footpaths, biking trails, and equestrian trails. The Sea Trail goes over mountain ridges down to Waddell State Beach on the coastline.

South of Boulder Creek on California Highway 9, watch for the forty-foot-high mural of actor James Dean at Brookdale Lodge. In the old resort, once a hideaway for Hollywood types, a babbling brook runs right through the dining room.

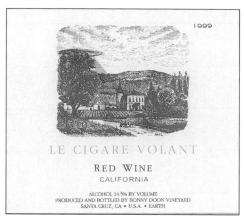

*The label of Bonny Doon's Le Cigare Volant—literally, "the flying cigar" in French—depicts a flying saucer beaming its rays on an unsuspecting vintner and his oxen.*

Off Quail Hollow Road near Ben Lomond is Quail Hollow Ranch County Park, a meadowy historic site where easy trails lead to the original ranch house, a pond inhabited by bass and bluegill, a shady picnic area, and a dwarf redwood forest. The park is home to the endangered Ben Lomond spineflower, an annual wildflower of the buckwheat family that blooms in small clusters of pale pink, six-petaled flowers and is found nowhere else in the world.

As you head up narrow, twisting Felton Empire Road, consider a stop at Hallcrest Vineyards and the Organic Wine Works, one of only a handful of vintners in the country making sulfite-free, certified organic wines. The Hall family planted Riesling vines here in 1941. From the sunny garden deck behind the old cottage, you can look out over the old vines while tasting a lush Santa Cruz Mountains Pinot Noir.

On Pine Flat Road off Empire Grade, Bonny Doon Vineyard was made famous by capricious labels such as Clos de Gilroy, Le Cigare Volant, and Old Telegram—fine wines produced by an irreverent owner and winemaker, Randall Grahm. Affectionately called the "Rhône Ranger," he was a maverick pioneer who bucked the Cabernet Sauvignon and Chardonnay trends of the early 1980s by experimenting with Rhône-style wines. Grahm's sturdy, aromatic Châteauneuf-du-Pape–style Rhône red is a blend of Grenache, Syrah, Mourvèdre, and Cinsault. Of the more than twenty extant Rhône varieties, nearly all are grown in this appellation. Duck under the winery's twig arbor to explore the path through a native plant garden and picnic under the trees.

In the Santa Cruz Mountains village of Felton, the Felton Covered Bridge soars thirty-four feet to the peak of its roof, making it the tallest in the United States. Erected in 1892, the bridge was tall enough to accommodate a fully loaded lumber wagon. Just downstream, the 180-foot Paradise Park Covered Bridge, built in 1872, spans the San Lorenzo River at the edge of the redwood preserve, Henry Cowell Redwoods State Park.

On the Yuba River near Nevada City is another of only a dozen covered bridges still standing in California. Resting on massive granite blocks, the 251-foot-long Bridgeport Covered Bridge is the longest single-span covered bridge in the United States––it is supported only at the two ends––and it may be the longest in the world, if measured by the roofline. In the 1860s, buggies and mule teams clattered across the floorboards beneath the same sugar-pine shingles and immense Douglas fir beams that you see today. In addition to the bridge, South Yuba River State Park has shady picnic spots and walking trails along the river and shallow wading pools among the river's rocks.

Built in 1863, Knights Ferry Covered Bridge near Oakdale stretches 355 feet across the Stanislaus River and is the longest multi-span covered bridge in the state. The skeleton of a large gristmill stands not far from the bridge, as do some "grinding stones" where Native Americans ground their acorns. Summer vacationers like to picnic and camp here by the river, wade, and launch their kayaks.

Bordering some of Bonny Doon's vineyards is a precious patch of wilderness, the northern section of Henry Cowell Redwoods State Park. A separate section of the park, just south of Felton, offers the opportunity to see rare first-growth redwoods and magnificent sycamores and pines in meadows and canyons on the San Lorenzo River and Eagle Creek. Even without trodding the trails you can get big views of Monterey Bay and the mountains from the observation deck.

Just south of Felton on Graham Hill Road, Roaring Camp is a re-creation of a logging camp, complete with covered bridge and general store, in a delightful forest setting. The narrow-gauge steam-powered train that once ferried lumber out of the mountains in the 1870s and 1880s now transports passengers, chugging up through redwood groves to the summit of Bear Mountain on the steepest railroad grade in North America. A second rail route runs along the San Lorenzo River down to Santa Cruz Beach.

## CARMEL VALLEY
### RANCHLANDS AND RESORTS, COWBOYS AND CABERNET

Rushing down steep canyons out of the wilds of the Santa Lucia Mountains, the Carmel River ambles over the floor of a narrow valley past pastures and palisades, equestrian estates and farms, before spilling into the Pacific Ocean. Visitors and vineyards enjoy the dry climate of the Carmel Valley, which is a world away from the bustling tourist towns of Carmel and Monterey and a warm retreat when fog blankets the coastline. Parts of the valley receive three hundred days of sunshine each year.

When they planted a backyard vegetable garden in Carmel Valley in 1984, former Manhattanites Myra and Drew Goodman had no inkling

## ROUTE 23

From California Highway 1 at Carmel, take Carmel Valley Road (County Road G16) southeast to Carmel Valley Village. Continue southeast, then take Tassajara Road west and Cachagua Road north to loop back to the village. Head north on Carmel Valley Road and Laureles Grade (County Road G20) to California Highway 68. Follow Highway 68 northwest to Olmstead Road. Take Olmstead Road and Jacks Peak Drive into Jacks Peak County Park.

that their Earthbound Farm would grow to twenty-four thousand acres and become North America's largest grower of certified organic produce. Lucky for travelers, the Earthbound Farm Stand on Carmel Valley Road is laden with organic fresh and dried fruits, herbs and vegetables, flowers, and healthy bakery goods. You are welcome to join harvest walks and chef-led tours in sixty acres of garden and to participate in garlic braiding and crafts workshops.

One of seven appellations making up Monterey County's diverse wine country, the Carmel Valley viticultural area favors the growing of Bordeaux-style varietals and Cabernet Sauvignon in particular. On Carmel Valley Road, Château Julien Wine Estate offers a complete winery and cellar tour with French ambiance. The estate welcomes visitors into a soaring, peak-roofed, stone-floored Great Hall, where a blaze in the fireplace lights up the stained-glass windows. Within the fifteen-inch-thick stone walls of the "Chai" house, the crisp *sur lie* Chardonnays and zesty Merlots and Cabernets age in oak barrels.

Cattle-ranching heritage is very much alive in the Carmel Valley, even though a few vacation resorts and the ever-expanding carpets of vineyards are encroaching on pasturelands. Western bands and cowboy poets hold forth at the annual California Cowboy Show. And at the Trail and Saddle Club, the California *vaquero* tradition of horsemanship, roping, and cattle working is taught and demonstrated by Ray Berta, who grew up in the saddle on a Carmel Valley ranch founded by his grandfather in the 1800s.

Mid-valley in Garland Ranch Regional Park, horseback riding and hiking trails amble through five thousand acres of oak savannah, through big leaf maple and pine groves, and up into a secluded redwood canyon. Snowmelt and spring rains flood waterfalls and fill the ponds, habitat for great blue herons, on the high mesa. Up here, views of the valley and the mountains are mesmerizing. From the back of a horse on a ridgetop trail ride, the historic country estate of Holman Ranch Equestrian Center looks much as it did when it was founded in 1928. Reminiscent of early Western landscape, it is often used as a film location for movies and television. The center is located just off Carmel Valley Road on Holman Road.

Outside the Running Iron Restaurant and Saloon in Carmel Valley Village, you may see motorcycles and bicycles, Jaguars and pickup trucks. Running Iron is the oldest continuously operating eating place in these parts, open since the 1940s. Cowboy boots and spurs hang from the ceiling, and steaks and south-of-the-border specialties are on the menu for local ranchers, winemakers, and tourists.

Among a grouping of wineries in the village, Heller Estate commands attention with a fifteen-foot-high bronze sculpture, entitled "Dancing Partners," at the entrance to a flamboyant sculpture garden. The winery's motto: "Magical Wines That Dance on Your Palate." Organically cultivated and dry farmed, the roots of the vines that produce Heller Cabernet Sauvignon reach deep into sandy soil, seeking moisture from the underground springs of the adjacent mountains' rugged Cachagua Valley.

When summertime temperatures in the Carmel Valley hover at the hundred-degree mark, it is cool at Galante Vineyards and Rose Gardens, where grapes, cattle, and fifteen thousand rose bushes thrive at 1,800 feet in elevation. Jack Galante—whose great grandfather was the founder of the town of Carmel—and his wife, Dawn, lure their friends, family, and other wine buffs up to their mountain hideaway on Cachagua Road for an annual "Days of Wine and Roses" festival during the clear, warm days of September. Fragrant rose petals cover the entrance road to the estate and live music, barbecue, winery and garden tours, and general merrymaking are on the agenda. When their dancing feet get hot and tired, partygoers sink them into tubs of cold water and rose petals.

Above Cachagua Road, the Los Padres Reservoir, created by the damming of the upper Carmel River, is a prime patch of water for trout fishing. Above the reservoir, the river's tributaries are habitat for pond turtles and endangered red-legged frogs. Off Cachagua Road at the end of Nason Road, you can find one of the trailheads for the Carmel River Trail and hike through the mountains all the way to Big Sur.

Heading out of Carmel Valley on Laureles Grade to California Highway 68, watch for a veritable wave of lavender in bloom in the spring and summer at Purple Pastures Lavender Farm.

For a walk in the wild to see ancient fossils and some native flora and fauna, stop at Jacks Peak County Park off Highway 68. Birders are on the lookout for pygmy nuthatches, chestnut-backed chickadees, and black-hooded, dark-eyed juncos among the wild sage, pines, and coyote brush. Not far from the park entrance is a display of fish, crab, and seashell fossils that were found here. The area was under the sea until about twelve million years ago, when an island and what is now Jacks Park began to emerge. The old seashore is exposed in an outcropping called the Aguajito Shale Formation, where several species of leaves, marine crustaceans, fish, and shells are still being unearthed.

## SALINAS VALLEY
## THE SALAD BOWL AND THE PINNACLES

Positioned between the golden Gabilan Mountains on the east and the wild Santa Lucia Range on the west, the sixty-mile-long, five-mile-wide Salinas Valley is called the "Salad Bowl of the World." Watered by the curling, twisting Salinas River, lettuce is a major crop, along with artichokes, strawberries, and other vegetables and fruits. Most of the strawberries and more than half of the broccoli and cauliflower produced in this country are grown here.

Going west from the town of Salinas, you will easily see the twenty-foot-tall, lifelike color figures of farmers, harvesting crews, and crop workers in the fields beside the highway. They are the unique art of John Cerney, who has been creating giant sculptures for more than three decades and installing them outdoors throughout Monterey County to draw attention to the value and humanity of farm workers. The roadside figures on California Highway

**ROUTE 24**

From Salinas, head west on California Highway 68 and south on River Road (County Road G17). Take a sidetrip onto Fort Romie Road. Returning to River Road, follow Foothill Road and Paraiso Springs Road south, Clark Road east, and Arroyo Seco Road south. Go east on Elm Avenue, crossing U.S. Highway 101 to Metz Road. Take Metz Road north to California Highway 146. From the highway, follow Stonewall Canyon to the west entrance of Pinnacles National Monument.

**ABOVE:**
*Horseback riding at Garland Ranch Regional Park is a great way to explore the wilds of the Carmel Valley.*

**RIGHT:**
*The region's cattle-ranching heritage is on display at the Roaring Iron Restaurant in Carmel Valley Village.*

**FACING PAGE, TOP:**
*Located high above the valley, the deck at Galante Vineyards is a prime spot for winding down after a day of touring.*

**FACING PAGE, BOTTOM:**
*Mist and sunbeams create a mystical scene among oak trees in the Carmel Valley.*

68 mark the location of The Farm, a large produce stand where you can learn about Salinas Valley agriculture by taking a guided tour in the fields to see and taste fresh vegetables and fruits.

Bicyclists and intrepid wine aficionados ply quiet River Road, meandering between agricultural lands to a few wineries and a unique animal farm. At Vision Quest Ranch, where over a hundred exotic animals and birds are lovingly trained for use in movie and television filming, you can take a tour to see elephants, giraffes, bears, cheetahs, tropical birds, snakes, alligators, and dozens more creatures, all glowing with health. Guests can stay overnight in canvas-walled safari cabins, and kids come to a summer camp for animal education.

Here in the Santa Lucia Highlands viticultural area on the west side of the valley, prehistoric glaciers and erosion left alluvial fans and benches, providing an exceptional *terroir* for Burgundian grape varietals—in particular, Chardonnay and Pinot Noir. Fogs off Monterey Bay sweep in during the growing season, burning off early in the morning. The vineyards warm significantly through the day until afternoon maritime breezes cool them off. Rain is scarce, and usually unknown from late winter until after harvest. This climate results in an especially long growing season, which allows the grapes to develop intense varietal character.

Take a short sidetrip on Fort Romie Road to see a small chapel and ruins of Mission Nuestra Señora de la Soledad. In 1791, a Spanish padre dedicated the thirteenth in the chain of California missions to Our Lady of Solitude, a name appropriate for what was then a desolate, sparsely populated location. A small museum contains vestments, early farming tools, dueling pistols, and photographs of Victorian-era farm families.

For the quintessential view of the Salinas Valley, stop by the breezy terrace at Smith and Hook Winery, off River Road on Foothill Road. In a little yellow house framed by century-old oaks, you can taste spicy Pinot Gris and Viognier, both redolent of apple and pear. The Merlot leans to bright cherry, with cinnamon and plum elements.

Heading into the foothills to Paraiso Vineyards, you know you are on a country road, as there is no center line. At the southern end of the appellation, an outdoor deck overlooks some of the seventeen different vineyard blocks

## FATHER SERRA'S MISSION

One of the most impressive in California's chain of Spanish missions, Mission San Carlos Borromeo de Carmelo was founded in 1770. Star-shaped stained-glass windows, cool colonnades, and courtyard gardens with bubbling fountains make this mission a pleasant retreat at the west end of the Carmel Valley.

A warren of thick, adobe-walled rooms hold a collection of early Native American, religious, and historical artifacts. Cool and silent even on the warmest days, the cathedral is painted in glowing tones of sienna, burnt umber, and gold. Under the altar is the burial place of Father Junipero Serra, the Spanish padre who founded eight of the state's missions and led the California Franciscans from his headquarters in Carmel until his death in 1784. From the mission, you can tread a footpath in the Mission Trail Nature Preserve, a small canyon of oak and Monterey pine.

planted on rugged slopes and canyons. The reasons to find this winery are its late-harvest Pinot Noir, the Souzao Port, and reserve wines are available only here.

From the sleepy farming community of Greenfield, art-loving travelers may head south on Central Avenue and west on Hobson Avenue to Scheid Vineyards. Housed in a restored century-old barn, the tasting room is colorful with Indonesian antiques and Mexican Talavera pottery. The labels of the bottles of Chardonnay, Merlot, and Pinot Noir have fascinating depictions of the works of Hong Kong–born artist, Dominic Man-Kit Lam. A former Harvard professor of biotechnology, Lam invented a process for creating mystical color images, reminiscent of Asian brush paintings, on black-and-white photographic paper. The term for the process, chromoskedasic painting, is derived from the Greek meaning "color by light scattering."

On the east side of the Salinas Valley, at California Highway 146 and Stonewall Canyon Road, right below the startling spires and steep cliffs of Pinnacles National Monument, is Chalone Vineyard. Its sloping Chardonnay and Pinot Noir vineyards experience dramatic daily temperature swings, as much as 40- to 60-degree changes in 24 hours, and even occasional snow in the winter. Rangers from Pinnacles National Monument lead the popular annual Chalone Vineyard Wildflower Walk from the winery, guiding hikers through fields of baby-blue-eyes, velvety pink mallow, California fuchsia and poppies, wild roses, magenta-colored shooting stars, and purple larkspur. These and dozens more varieties of flora make the Pinnacles one of the loveliest places to be in the springtime.

The park is a paradise for rock climbers, who scramble up steep canyon walls and domes. Hiking trails lead to ferny creeks, a swimming hole, spooky caves, and big views of the valley and the Gabilan Mountains. Endangered juvenile California condors have been released here, and they appear to be thriving. Seeing a condor, with its wingspan of nearly ten feet, hovering overhead in the wind or perched on a stone column drying its wings in the sun can be an unforgettable experience.

## STEINBECK'S WORLD

Born and raised in Salinas, John Steinbeck lived there and on the nearby Monterey Peninsula until his forties. Drawing on his Salinas Valley heritage, he wrote about the struggles and romances of early farm families, migrant laborers, and Dust Bowl migrants in his Pulitzer Prize– and Nobel Prize–winning books, *Cannery Row, Tortilla Flat, East of Eden,* and *The Grapes of Wrath,* among others.

To honor their most famous of citizens, the city of Salinas erected an expansive, interactive, glass-walled monolith of a museum, the National Steinbeck Center, where you can experience some of the sights, sounds, and smells of Steinbeck's stories and his life in Salinas. Pull out a drawer to see his childhood treasures. Feel the chill of an "ice-packed" boxcar filled with lettuce, and get a glimpse of migrant life in the Salinas Valley. Movies based on Steinbeck stories are playing, and visitors can walk through doors and peer through windows at historic vignettes and into Steinbeck's charming camper truck, in which he motored with his dog and wrote *Travels with Charley.*

A few blocks away, visitors can explore his boyhood home, the Steinbeck House, an elaborately decorated Victorian loaded with memorabilia.

**ABOVE:**
*The Sierra de Salinas, the mountain range seen here looming beyond the vineyards, forms the western edge of the Salinas Valley.*

**FACING PAGE, CLOCKWISE FROM TOP LEFT:**
*Picnicking at the Smith and Hook Winery is a quintessential wine-country experience.*

*After decades of neglect, the adobe Mission Nuestra Señora de la Soledad has been restored to its original eighteenth-century elegance.*

*Built in 1797, Mission San Juan Bautista may be best known for its part in the Alfred Hitchcock film* Vertigo, *although the bell tower in the climactic scene was constructed by the movie studio for the film.*

*Part of the San Juan Bautista State Historic Park, the Plaza Hotel looks more or less as it did in the stagecoach days, when it was a popular stopover for miners and traders traveling along the coast.*

# SAN JUAN BAUTISTA
## EARLY CALIFORNIA HISTORY,
## SAN BENITO COUNTY WINES

### ROUTE 25

From San Juan Bautista, drive southeast on California Highway 156 to Union Road. Follow Union to Cienega Road, and take Cienega south to explore the wineries of the Cienega Valley. Retrace the route to return to San Juan Bautista, or continue on Cienega Road to California Highway 25, following it south to the east entrance of Pinnacles National Monument.

A Spanish village in the late 1700s, and not much larger now, the little town of San Juan Bautista consists of a large state historic park, a mission cathedral, and a few charming streets of antique shops and Mexican restaurants shaded with overhanging pepper, mimosa, and black walnut trees. On quiet farm roads, a few wineries produce remarkable wines in the Cienega Valley, Lime Kiln Valley, and Mount Harlan appellations.

Anchoring San Juan Bautista around a grassy plaza are museums in historic adobes, Victorian-era buildings, and the largest of Father Junipero Serra's California missions. Built in 1797, Mission San Juan Bautista has three aisles, and the forty-foot-high ceiling of giant beams reflects the traditional *viga-latilla* formation of Spanish architecture. Daylight floods the cathedral, highlighting the vivid rust and blue painted decoration. Surrounding the church are the padres' former living quarters, which house a museum of early Native American, Spanish Colonial, and Victorian artifacts, including one of the best collections of Mission-style furniture in the world. The mission gardens are rampant with giant cacti, aromatic lavender, and climbing roses, and behind the church under ancient olive trees, more than four thousand Native Americans and early pioneers are buried. The cemetery and the plaza overlook fields of row crops and the San Andreas earthquake fault, here at the south end of the Santa Cruz Mountains. A seismograph sits in a glass box, recording every tremor.

Bordering the San Juan Bautista State Historic Park greensward, which fronts the mission, are historic buildings, barns, hotels, and homes. Carriages, wagons, and stagecoaches recall the 1860s, when seven stage lines ran through here between San Francisco and Los Angeles, loaded with silver and gold miners and traders. The restored adobe Plaza Hotel was the first place the dusty travelers headed, for beer or something stronger in the saloon. The hotel owner, Angelo Zanetta, built himself a magnificent dwelling, Plaza Hall, which today displays early California furnishings. The red-tile-roofed Castro House was owned by a survivor of the ill-fated Donner party; behind the house, a fat-trunked, 150-year-old pepper tree shades lovely gardens.

As premium wineries are new ventures in San Benito County, and their wines lesser known than most, few people are aware of the wine and wilderness adventures to be had in the San Juan Bautista area and around Hollister, just to the southeast. On Cienega Road in the Cienega Valley, three wineries wait to be discovered in the rolling hills at the foot of Mount Harlan. Each has singular attractions in addition to their fine wines.

On the drive to the Pietra Santa Winery, you will pass a 1906 Frank Lloyd Wright–designed house, several thousand olive trees, and a bocce ball court before arriving at an impressive Tuscan-style villa with antique Italian roof tiles. The owner, Joseph Gimelli, is an Italian American; the winemaker,

Alessio Carli, is a native of Siena, Italy, and formerly a winemaker at one of Tuscany's legendary Chianti estates, Badia a Coltibuono. Together they produce the Vache line of wines, named for the French immigrant, Theophile Vache, who was the first to plant vineyards in the Cienega Valley, in 1850. In the Old World–style tasting room, you can sip Sangiovese, Pinot Grigio, and a unique Dolcetto, and try the Pietra Santa estate olive oils.

In their gunmetal gray buildings right on top of the San Andreas earthquake fault, father and son DeRose welcome visitors to DeRose Vineyards. Some of their Zinfandel comes from vines planted in the late 1890s. Together with the Viogner, the Zinfandel vines are dry farmed in the deep sandy-loam soils of terraced hillsides with no irrigation. The bold, dark Hollywood Red table wine is named for a 1940 Graham Hollywood, one of several perfectly restored antique cars on display here. From vines over a century old, the DeRose Negrette, usually known as Pinot St. George in the United States, is a rare wine to come across even where it originates, in France. This earthy, spicy, plumy Rhône-style concoction is worth the drive.

At 2,200 feet in elevation, a thirty-foot-tall limekiln marks the property of the Calera Wine Company, where limestone was quarried a century or so ago. The owner and winemaker, Josh Jensen, attended Oxford University in England, then worked harvests in Burgundy and the Rhône Valley in France before returning home to California to seek out the perfect limestone-rich soil in which to plant Pinot Noir. Stumbling upon an abandoned limestone quarry, he planted his vineyards on the slopes of Mount Harlan, where marine breezes, low rainfall, and the limestone soil create a *terroir* similar to Burgundy's Côte d'Or. The Calera vineyards are the only ones in the tiny Mount Harlan viticultural area. Jensen's dark ruby, intensely flavored Pinots have achieved cult status among oenophiles.

Calera *is Spanish for "limekiln," and the well-preserved, thirty-foot-tall masonry calera near the Calera Wine Company vineyard is featured on every bottle.*

# PART VI

# SOUTHERN WINE ROADS:
## WESTERN TOWNS AND RHÔNE REDS

**FACING PAGE:**
*Mission Santa Inez near Solvang is an active parish today, more than two hundred years after its construction.*

**ABOVE:**
*Just a few miles from the coast, the Edna Valley has an ideal climate for producing wines such as these offerings from the Edna Valley Vineyard.*

At the same time that American colonists were rebelling against England, Spaniards were building outposts in the coastal valleys of Alta California. The conquistadors galloped through the Santa Ynez and Santa Maria River valleys and the Paso Robles area, camping under massive valley oaks in wild stream canyons. Falling in love with the seductive contours of the golden land, the moderate climate, and the natural riches of flora and fauna, they stayed, establishing sprawling ranchos.

When Spanish priests arrived to build a chain of mission churches along El Camino Real from San Diego north, they carried with them mustard seed from their homeland and planted it to mark the trails. Today, yellow mustard is a harbinger of spring in the vineyards of Santa Barbara and San Luis Obispo counties. Spring is a good time of year to explore the backroads—the valleys are fresh and green and wildflowers are in bloom, and it is before the hot days and the influx of vacationers in the summertime.

Among cow pastures and horse-breeding farms, wheat fields and row crops, vineyards are gradually multiplying. Cool, misty nights and mornings; warm, dry days; and an east-west orientation make these valleys similar to those in the Rhône district of France. The influence of the Pacific Ocean breezes and lower temperatures give grapes a long "hang time"—perfect conditions for Chardonnays, peppery Syrahs, and the rich, dark Pinot Noirs known as "Rhône reds."

At many of the family-owned wineries, the proprietors or winemakers themselves will welcome you to their small, barn-board tasting rooms. On weekdays, you may be among just a handful of guests.

Besides wine adventures in the southern wine valleys, expect a clutch of tiny western villages, some hot springs resorts and country inns, historic missions, dude ranches, a Danish-style tourist's town, and sylvan walking trails.

## PASO ROBLES
### COWBOY COUNTRY

Settling in the foothills below the dark ridgeline of the Santa Lucia Mountains in the late 1700s, Spanish Franciscan padres built Mission San Miguel Arcángel and planted grapes for their sacramental wines. Decades later, when the Mexican army occupied the area, a land grant called El Paso de Robles—"the pass of the oaks"—was purchased for eight thousand dollars by the Blackburn and James families. In the 1860s, the Southern Pacific Railroad arrived, and the small town of Paso Robles began to grow as headquarters for farmers and ranchers. The town's carefully preserved late-nineteenth-century and early twentieth-century buildings feature a range of architectural styles and today house a lively mix of restaurants, shops, and residences.

More than eighty wineries and over two hundred vineyards thrive within the Paso Robles appellation. Twenty miles inland from the Pacific Ocean, the variation in temperatures is dramatic, with summer days over one hundred degrees and nighttime lows in winter dipping below freezing,

ROUTE 26

From Paso Robles, take California Highway 46E east as far as Tobin James Winery. Reverse direction and follow Highway 46E west, stopping at wineries along the way. Cross U.S. Highway 101 to Adelaida Road, which runs west to Vineyard Drive. At the intersection of Adelaida and Vineyard, a short detour north on Chimney Rock Road will take you to Justin Vineyards. Return to Vineyard Drive and head east to Templeton. Cross U.S. Highway 101, and follow Templeton Road east to Wild Horse Winery.

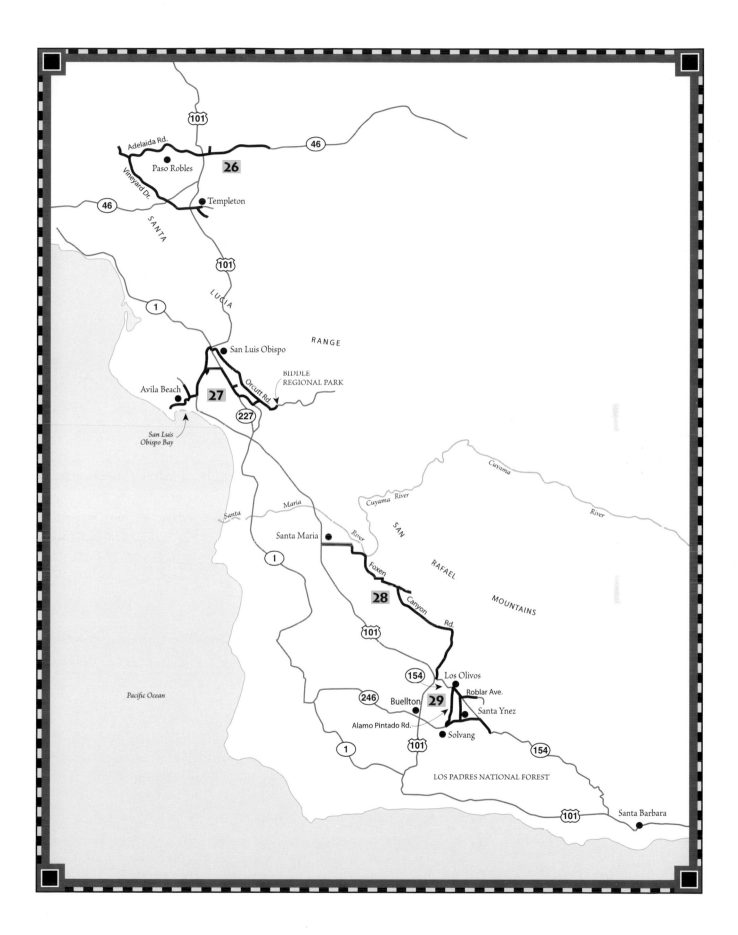

*Mission San Miguel Arcángel, founded in 1797, was the sixteenth of the twenty-one Spanish missions along California's El Camino Real (The Royal Highway).*

with little rain during the growing season. Cool coastal breezes flow over the Santa Lucia mountain range to cool the vineyards most evenings. Warm-climate reds such as Zinfandel, Cabernet Sauvignon, Merlot, and Rhône-style varieties constitute about 80 percent of the grapes grown here in stony, chalky soil.

In the low hills east of Palo Robles, Tobin James Cellars harvests Zinfandel grapes from a forty-acre plot of head-pruned, dry-farmed vineyards first planted in 1924. Formerly a stagecoach stop, the winery looks more like a Western saloon than a modern tasting room. Visitors are loudly welcomed up to a rococo, circa-1860 mahogany bar that was shipped from Blue Eye, Missouri. While kids play arcade games, their parents sip and snap photos of Western memorabilia, from six-shooters to saddles, lariats, and horse collars.

A mile or so west on California Highway 46E, Meridian Vineyards is surrounded by a luxuriant herb garden and a grove of ancient oak trees. You can rest here on a bench among the hummingbirds, finches, and frogs, amid the pungent scent of sage and rosemary, and have a picnic overlooking a reservoir and rows of vines.

Roses line the grand entrance to EOS Estate Winery at Arciero Estate Vineyards. The Romanesque-style stone edifice is meant to be reminiscent of Montecassino, a Benedictine monastery near the winery owner's Italian hometown of Santa Elia Fiumerapido. Besides traditional Paso Robles appellation varieties, EOS produces a unique late-harvest Moscato called "Tears of Dew" and a dated Zinfandel port.

Giant boulders crowd the entrance of cool underground cellars at Eberle Winery. Gary Eberle pioneered San Luis Obispo County winemaking, planting Syrah cuttings brought from France on his Estrella River benchlands in the mid-1970s.

Another pioneer in the industry, Martin and Weyrich Winery, on Buena Vista Drive just off Highway 46, was the first in the state to create "Cal-Italia" varietal wines, such as Nebbiolo and Sangiovese. Old-vine Zinfandels are produced from dry-farmed vineyards on the west side of the appellation. Affiliated with the winery, Villa Toscana is a small, luxurious inn just up the road. Cloistered walkways, a campanile, rough-hewn beams, and fancy ironwork create the ambience of an estate in Tuscany.

West of Paso Robles is that part of the appellation called the Adelaida, or the "Far Out" wineries region. Not far from the coastline, in rough, rocky terrain and varying elevations and microclimates, a few premium wineries hold forth. Just north of our route on Chimney Rock Road, Justin Vineyards and Winery welcomes visitors for cave tours and tastings of its singular "Isosceles"-style Cabernets, Syrahs, and Rhône varietals, and its unique Mourvedres and Malbec varietals.

When the Mexican army occupied California in the 1820s, it granted expansive ranchos to various local worthies, who established cattle ranches and grain farms. By 1886, the Southern Pacific Railroad was shipping cattle out of the hamlet of Templeton, which began to grow as a supply headquarters and gathering place for the surrounding area. Today's reminders of the agricultural and ranching history are the huge Templeton Feed and Grain silo, smack in the middle of town, and the Templeton Livestock Market, where real cowboys buy and sell horses and cattle and participate in penning and roping competitions.

At the Templeton Tavern, you may find yourself elbow to elbow with a cowpuncher in riding boots or a vineyard worker in a wine-stained shirt. Down the Main Street, Herrmann's Chocolate Lab and Ice Cream Parlor draws both tourists and Templeton families. A general store and a bank in the 1880s, the A. J. Spurs restaurant building is crowded with Old West memorabilia, including cowhides, spurs, horse collars, and vintage photographs.

One of a handful of small wineries near Templeton, Wild Horse Winery on Templeton Road is named for the wild mustangs in the hills, the descendants of the first horses introduced to California by the Spanish in the later 1700s.

## HOT SPRINGS

The Salinan Indians and Spanish mission padres knew the Paso Robles area as Agua Caliente, meaning "hot water," referring to the many natural underground hot mineral springs. As early as the 1860s, spas and mud baths in the town were tourist attractions and "taking the waters" a popular pastime. The original Paso Robles Hot Springs Hotel was built in 1864. It was replaced, after a few incarnations, in 1942 by the Paso Robles Inn, which today draws the healing waters into aromatic—think sulphur—whirlpool tubs on private patios overlooking a lush garden.

Another historic spa, Sycamore Mineral Springs Resort, between Paso Robles and Avila, has been a popular destination since 1897 and remains a tranquil retreat. You can arrange to soak in hot, mineral-rich waters in a tub secluded in the woods, explore the extensive gardens along Lopez Creek, or take a stroll on a paved footpath that leads to Avila Beach.

Also on the way to Avila, nestled against a forested hillside, Avila Valley Hot Springs maintains a huge, heated swimming pool and a mineral pool fed by 105-degree water from an artesian well. The mild, marine climate and ocean breezes keep this corner of the valley twenty degrees cooler in summer and twenty degrees warmer in winter than locations just a mile or two inland.

**RIGHT:**
*The Eberle Winery was one of the first, and most successful, wineries in San Luis Obispo County.*

**BELOW:**
*The luxuriant gardens alone make the Justin Vineyards and Winery a worthy detour west of Paso Robles.*

**ABOVE:**
San Luis Bay is peaceful in the morning light, as seen from the village of Shell Beach.

**LEFT:**
Plenty of country gifts are to be had at Avila Valley Barn, near Avila Beach.

# EDNA VALLEY
## LAND OF CHARDONNAY

### ROUTE 27

From U.S. Highway 101 on the south end of San Luis Obispo, take Los Osos Valley Road east and Higuera Street north to Tank Farm Road, which runs east to California Highway 227. Follow Highway 227 south. Take a left on Biddle Ranch Road to Edna Valley Vineyard; reverse direction and continue south on Highway 227 to Corbett Canyon Road. From Corbett Canyon, follow Tiffany Ranch Road east to Orcutt Road. To reach Talley Vineyards and Biddle Regional Park, head south on Orcutt Road and east on Lopez Drive. Return to Orcutt Road and head north to Broad Street. Go north on Broad Street to U.S. 101. Drive south on U.S. 101 and west on San Luis Bay Drive. Take a right to drive up See Canyon Road; come back and continue west on San Luis Bay Drive to Avila Beach Drive, which will lead you to the beach.

Midway between northern and southern California, just four miles from the Pacific Ocean, the first grapevines in the Edna Valley were planted in the late 1870s by homesteading pioneers. Some of their Zinfandel vineyards still exist today. Afternoon sea breezes funnel through the four-mile-wide valley, lowering summer temperatures and allowing a long season for the grapes to develop the intense, complex flavors of the famous Edna Valley Chardonnays, Pinot Noirs, Syrahs, and white Rhône varietals.

The best view of the Edna Valley is from the tasting room and terrace of Edna Valley Vineyard on Biddle Ranch Road. From here, you can see a jagged parade of dark, pointed mountains called the "Seven Sisters," a chain of fifty-million-year-old volcanic plug domes called "morros." The last morro is Morro Rock, the California version of the Rock of Gibraltar; it is a craggy 576-foot-tall peak at the mouth of the natural estuary of Morro Bay.

The frost-free, dry climate and twenty-five-million-year-old volcanic and marine deposits in the valley's subsoil create a *terroir* that produces the crisp mineral nuances of this appellation's Chardonnays. One of the oldest wineries in the state, Edna Valley Vineyard is famous for Chardonnay, some made of fruit from twenty-five-year-old vines. The luscious wine has been described as tasting of white peach and citrus, with a long, mineral fullness.

Driving along the highway, it's hard to miss the Old Edna sign on a striking, silvery building, which is now a welcome roadside stop for local winery workers and travelers. The tiny township of Edna boomed in the nineteenth century, but by the 1930s, Edna and its businesses waned. Eventually, all the buildings except a barn, the railroad depot, and Edna Hall either burned down or crumbled. At the turn of this century, Pattea Torrence purchased Edna Hall and the acreage around it, restoring the building and installing an art gallery, called In the Tin. She leases the ground floor to Fiala's Gourmet Deli, Espresso Bar, and Chocolatier. She has also renovated country cottages and opened the Suite Edna Bed and Breakfast.

On Corbett Canyon Road, look for the vintage tractor on the roadside marking the tasting room at Kynsi Winery, housed in a restored 1940s dairy. Its vineyard-designated Syrah was named "Best Syrah in California" at the state fair, and its "Merrah" blend of Syrah and Merlot is entirely unique.

Before turning north on Orcutt Road, consider a walk or a picnic under huge old sycamores and oaks at Biddle Regional Park. The park can be accessed by driving south on Orcutt Road and east on Lopez Drive. It is here that wineries and restaurants set up tents for the Grand Tasting at the annual Wine Harvest Celebration in November. Also on Lopez Drive is Talley Vineyards, at the entrance of which is the El Rincon adobe, a two-story structure built in 1863.

Keep your eyes peeled for Baileyana Winery, housed in the one-room, yellow Independence Schoolhouse that was built for Edna Valley kids in 1909. You'll find it on Orcutt Road past the intersection with Biddle Ranch Road. Close your eyes and inhale the black cherry and boysenberry aromas of the ruby-colored Pinot Noir. Valley views are lovely from here, and you can linger for a game of croquet or bocce ball.

West of U.S. Highway 101 off Avila Beach Drive, the Avila Valley is a miniature wine region with country-style attractions. At Apple Valley Barn, sample fresh-pressed cider and some of seventy varieties of local apples; taste local honeys, home-baked pastries, and pies; and pick your own olallieberries and raspberries. Kids love the pygmy goats, hayrides, and picnics under the trees. While here, pick up some Avila Valley Schoolhouse Cellars apple wine, made from heirloom apples grown in the sheltered arroyos of See Canyon.

A mile up See Canyon Road, a lane quiet enough for walking or biking, Kelsey See Canyon Vineyards greets visitors with an old Model T loaded with wine barrels. Dick and Delores Kelsey make Apple Chardonnay, a silky late-harvest Zinfandel, and a sweet Orange Muscat dessert wine, among others.

The village of Avila Beach on San Luis Bay is in a slow recovery from decades as an oil terminal, where oceangoing tankers from around the world picked up oil from inland wells. The entire downtown was razed and the underlying sand decontaminated. Now the calm harbor, fishing pier, and small beaches are surrounded by a handful of inns, cafés, and shops.

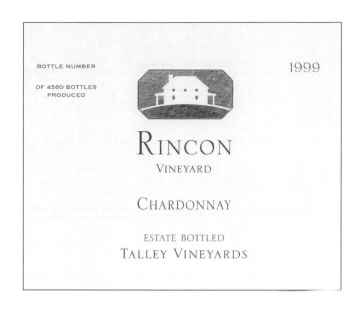

*The historic Rincon adobe stands at the entrance to the Talley Vineyards estate, and it appears on the label of every Chardonnay, Sauvignon Blanc, Pinot, and other wines from Talley's Rincon Vineyard.*

## SANTA BARBARA COUNTY
### FOXEN CANYON WINE TRAIL

A twenty-mile stretch of hilly terrain between the Santa Maria and Santa Ynez valleys, Foxen Canyon Road winds through a sylvan setting inhabited by grazing longhorn steer, thoroughbred horses, and old windmills spinning in the breeze. The area's centuries-old tradition of agriculture and cattle raising began a transformation in the 1970s when wine grape vineyards began to appear. A mere two hundred acres of planted vines marked the birth of the entire winemaking region, and the innovative owners of Firestone Vineyard, Rancho Sisquoc, Santa Barbara, and Zaca Mesa forged a future for Santa Barbara County wines.

A modern Spanish-style villa, Firestone Vineyard's winery on Zaca Station Road overlooks Zaca Canyon. A vivid mural, photos, and artifacts document the founding of the enterprise by Leonard K. Firestone, former

**ROUTE 28**

Between Buellton and Los Alamos, just north of the junction of U.S. Highway 101 and California Highway 154, take Zaca Station Road north to Foxen Canyon Road. Follow Foxen Canyon Road northwest to Betteravia Road, which runs west to U.S. 101.

*Foxen Canyon Road winds through the verdant hills and fields of Santa Barbara County.*

*Northwest of Santa Barbara, the Santa Maria Valley only recently converted from traditional agriculture and ranching to grape vineyards.*

**ABOVE:**
*The tasting room at the Firestone Vineyard is adorned with murals and photos chronicling the Firestone family's legacy in winemaking.*

**LEFT:**
*The Rancho Sisquoc Winery is set in a quiet wooded area in the foothills of the San Rafael Mountains.*

chairman of the Firestone Tire and Rubber Company, and his son, Brooks. The legacy continues with the younger generation, Adam and Andrew Firestone. Among their singular wines, the darkly intense Syrah hints of blackberry and mocha, violets and white pepper. The fresh, fruity Rieslings are steady gold-medal winners, achieving "Best Riesling" at the state fair.

Down the road apiece, the television star of *Davy Crockett* and *Daniel Boone* fame in the 1950s and 1960s, Fess Parker, has his own winery. He is often found signing autographs and pouring wine at Fess Parker Winery, a copper-roofed, Australian-style ranch house in a tall meadow. Besides Syrahs, Chardonnays, and Pinots, Parker makes dry Rieslings and a luscious golden dessert wine, Muscat Canelli.

Look for the windmill at the entrance to Zaca Mesa Winery, one of the first in the county to plant the Syrah grape, and the training ground for some of region's greatest winemakers. Plummy, spicy, leathery, and elegant are some of the words used to describe the Zaca Mesa Syrahs and the exotic varietals Roussanne, Viognier, and Mourvedre. After a visit to the low-slung, wooden farm building that serves as a tasting room, you can picnic on a high knoll under the oaks and take a short walk on a meadow trail. A huge chessboard awaits players, who move the three-foot-high pieces around the courtyard.

In 1837, English sea captain William Benjamin Foxen purchased a Spanish land grant, Rancho Tinaquaic. His descendants—farmers and ranchers—have owned this land continuously, and in 1987, his great-great-grandson, Dick Doré and his partner, Bill Wathen, established Foxen Winery and Vineyard. Visitors are welcomed at a barnlike former blacksmith shop on the roadside—a building that typifies the rusticity of many small tasting rooms in the appellation.

In addition to harvesting their own grapes, Foxen buys grapes grown in one the most prestigious vineyards in the world, the Bien Nacido Vineyard. Bien Nacido is a nine-hundred-acre plot on what is called the Santa Maria Bench, perched at one thousand feet in elevation on a south-facing slope below the Sierra Madre Mountains. On Santa Maria Mesa Road, just north of our route, you can actually drive right between the rows of grapevines, which are lined up on a plateau below the soft shoulders of the foothills. The road's wide views of the valley and its canyons are breathtaking.

When you see the century-old, two-steepled San Ramon Chapel on Foxen Canyon Road, turn into the drive leading to Rancho Sisquoc Winery. Above the Sisquoc River, a compound of white farm buildings is surrounded by green pastures, walnut, olive, and fig trees, and some three hundred acres of vineyards. At the foot of a steep, wooded cliff is the redwood and stone tasting room, where wine lovers taste and buy Chardonnay, Sauvignon Blanc, and Cabernet Sauvignon while enjoying the view from the picnic grounds under mossy oaks. This warm, eastern corner of the Santa Maria Valley viticultural area, a 3,200-acre district around the Santa Maria Bench, has been proposed to receive its own AVA designation.

Horse breeding, cow punching, and ranching have been the heritage of southern California coastal valleys since the Spanish galloped up from Mexico in the eighteenth century. Arabians, thoroughbreds, German Trakehners, and Icelandic horses, framed by white fences, make for picturesque tableaus along the backroads. An attraction for horse lovers near Solvang, Flag Is Up Farms is owned by Monty Roberts, the "Horse Whisperer" made famous in the movie of the same name. On weekends, he demonstrates his nonviolent training techniques for visitors.

More than seventy miniature horses, each no more than thirty-five inches tall, are on view at Quicksilver Miniature Horse Ranch on Alama Pintado Road between Solvang and Ballard. Once bred in the 1600s by European royalty, the animals were imported to the United States in the 1930s to work in coal mines. Today's sweet-natured minis are bred for pets and for show.

The Alisal Guest Ranch and Resort is a ten-thousand-acre working cattle and horse ranch. Its history dates to 1843 when Spanish conquistador Raimundo Carillo received a land grant from the Mexican government and became the first cattle rancher in the Santa Ynez Valley. Today, following a tradition set by Hollywood stars Doris Day, Clark Gable, and others, guests hide away in cottages shaded by sycamores, play golf, cast for trout in a spring-fed lake, and choose their mounts from more than a hundred quarter horses.

In Los Olivos, the Wilding Art Museum exhibits equestrian and Western art, including paintings of early days in the valley. In Santa Ynez, nearly four hundred horseshoes are inlaid in the pavement, and vintage California tack, saddles, and harnesses are on display in the Santa Ynez Valley Historical Museum.

Annual equestrian-related events include rodeos in Santa Maria and Santa Barbara, a countywide polo season, and the Vaquero Show in Santa Ynez.

## SANTA YNEZ VALLEY
### A SPANISH MISSION, SYRAHS, AND SALOONS

A modern version of an old Danish village, complete with gas-lit streetlamps and windmills, Solvang makes a good launching pad for tours of the Santa Ynez and Santa Maria valleys. At the east end of town, stop at Mission Santa Inez (or Inés) to tour the nicely restored and colorfully painted interior of the mission church, which was founded in 1804 by Spanish padres who aimed to convert the local Chumash Indians. Native American artists painted the wall murals and the floor tiles, while European art and sculpture recall the church's Spanish heritage.

One of only two mountain ranges running directly east-west along the 1,100-mile California coastline, the Santa Ynez Mountains are a perfect funnel for fog blown in by steady breezes from the Pacific. This microclimate of cool nights and mornings and warm, dry days is perfect for peppery Syrahs, intense, dark Pinot Noirs, and sensuous Chardonnays. These wines are produced by a handful of premium wineries scattered in a triangle, called the Santa Ynez Wine Trail, between Solvang and the tiny western towns of Santa Ynez and Los Olivos.

**ROUTE 29**

From Solvang, take California Highway 246 east to Alamo Pintado Road; drive north on Alamo Pintado to Los Olivos. Head southeast on California Highway 154, then go east on Roblar Avenue. Return west on Roblar, cross Highway 154, and turn south on Refugio Road to Santa Ynez. Take Highway 246 east to Highway 154, and continue southeast on Highway 154 over the San Marcos Pass to Santa Barbara.

**FACING PAGE, CLOCKWISE FROM TOP:**
*Located in the Danish-inspired village of Solvang, the Wine Valley Inn is a short drive from dozens of Santa Barbara County wineries.*

*This old car in Santa Ynez has seen better days.*

*One of the many quaint shops along the main street of Los Olivos.*

**ABOVE:**
*A tractor sits lonely in the field at sunrise near Refugio Road in Santa Ynez.*

155

Between Solvang and Los Olivos, take a slow ramble on Alamo Pintado Road. Among the historic buildings on this rural route is a 1926 Craftsman farmhouse that serves as the tasting room at Foley Estates Winery. One of the signature wines estate-bottled here, the Sauvignon Blanc is crafted in a bold Chardonnay style to produce a marriage of melon, fig, and tropical fruit flavors mingled with the mysterious aroma of tea.

Nearby, in a grove of magnificent old oaks, is the rare, two-story 1884 adobe of Rideau Vineyard. Graciously appealing, the vineyard has Adirondack chairs and picnic tables in the gardens, New Orleans jazz, and, occasionally, Creole cooking in the tasting room.

A 1918 flagpole stands guard in the one-horse town of Los Olivos, which was used as the set for the TV series *Mayberry RFD*. Lining the main street are clapboard buildings, some from the 1800s, housing upscale art galleries, antiques shops, and wine-tasting rooms. Kahn Winery boasts the smallest tasting room in the state—nothing more than a tiny log cabin. Kahn christened its Cabernet Franc "Cab Frank," in honor of Frank Sinatra. His music is played at every stage of the winemaking process to infuse the wine with the smooth sounds, and the labels feature paintings by Sinatra.

If the wisteria-draped Los Olivos Café seems familiar, it may be because some of the scenes in the 2005 movie *Sideways* were filmed here. Dozens of Santa Barbara wines are available by the glass and the bottle to accompany inventive California-Mediterranean cuisine.

On the edge of town, a cavernous white building was the stagecoach stop in the 1880s. These days at Brothers Restaurant at Mattei's (pronounced "Matty's"), locals cut loose on open mike night, while travelers lounge in armchairs by a river-rock hearth, perusing the tavern's original guest book and photos of bygone days.

On meandering roads east of town are tasting rooms and wineries galore. On Roblar Avenue, a lane lined with century-old olive trees, Clairmont Farms grows rows and rows of lavender. For a heady experience of fragrance and color, and lovely valley views, come before the harvest in late summer to choose from oils, lotions, bundles of lavender, and even aromatic dog shampoo. Down the road, Bridlewood Estate Winery impresses passersby with dramatic Mission-style architecture and lush landscaping. Just beyond the winery is the entrance gate to Sedgwick Reserve, where trails and rushing creeks thread through the grounds of an old ranch and pristine backwoods at the foot of Figueroa Mountain. In elevations from 800 to 2,300 feet, verdant woods, savanna, and riparian habitats—and some endangered vernal pools—shelter wildlife, including bobcats and dozens of bird species. The precious reserve is a University of California research site and open to the public for guided hikes.

Located on Refugio Road (off Roblar Avenue), among poplars, cottonwoods, and redwoods is the steep-roofed, pink French-style building of Brander Vineyards. Inside, the vineyard offers Sauvignon Blanc and such other wines as Bouillabaisse Rosé, Dos Mundos Malbec, Bouchet, and Tête de Cuvée, a dark, sassy award winner with a cassis-cherry aroma.

In the rustic little burg of Santa Ynez, a good place to hear gossip and hang out with the locals (who are often movie stars living on the horse ranches nearby) is the Maverick Saloon, which looks like an old Western movie set, complete with dollar bills on the ceiling and grizzled cowpokes at the long bar.

Tucked away in a voluptuous Victorian garden, the Santa Ynez Inn is a dramatic departure from the Wild West rusticity of the town. Behind curlicue balconies and bubbling fountains is a two-story mansion with marble fireplaces, canopied beds, and lavish trappings—one of the most luxurious, and private, hostelries in southern California.

Heading out of Santa Ynez on the way to Santa Barbara, California Highway 154 winds up through eucalyptus and manzanita into the Los Padres National Forest, topping out at San Marcos Pass, a thousand feet above the valley. Travelers in the know save time for refreshments or a meal at Cold Spring Tavern at the top of the pass. Over a hundred years ago, rattling stagecoaches stopped here at the Cold Spring Relay Station to change teams of horses and allow their travelers to rest and eat. On weekends, the tavern can be packed wall to wall with day-trippers from the city, cowboys, and Harley riders, all kicking back with beer and platters of beefsteak, venison, and buffalo, while live bluegrass music or a blues band makes Monday morning seem a world away.

Leaving the tavern, you get a bird's-eye view of the Cold Spring Canyon Arched Bridge, one of the longest arched steel bridges in the country, spanning four hundred feet above the gaping canyon.

## SIDEWAYS IN SANTA RITA

Two seekers of midlife enlightenment and sublime Pinot Noir—the main characters of the 2005 movie *Sideways*, which was filmed almost entirely in the Santa Barbara wine country—began their saga west of U.S. Highway 101 in the Santa Rita Hills appellation. In the movie, a long-haired, bearded, cowboy-hat-wearing denizen of the valley holds forth in the tasting room of Sanford Winery on Santa Rosa Road.

Richard Sanford and Pierre Lafond of Lafond Winery and Vineyards were the first to grow Burgundian-style grapes here in the early 1970s, but it was more than two decades before wine critics began to take note. Medal winners now, Sanford wines tend to crispness and mineral austerity, elements characteristic of the Santa Rita grapes grown in the flinty chert soils between the green folds of the Purisima Hills and the Santa Rosa Hills.

Sanford Winery visitors may see red-tailed hawks and rescued, endangered peregrine falcons, which are released on the property, and a pristine creek canyon thick with redwoods, sycamores, and willows. Believed to be the largest handmade adobe building erected since the California missions were built, the winery was built of handmade adobe blocks and recycled Douglas fir timbers from an old sawmill.

# INDEX

# ABOUT THE AUTHOR AND PHOTOGRAPHER

## KAREN MISURACA

Karen Misuraca is a travel, golf, and outdoor writer from Sonoma, in the California wine country. She is the award-winning author of *The California Coast* as well as *Our San Francisco, The 100 Best Golf Resorts of the World, Fun with the Family Northern California, Quick Escapes from San Francisco,* and other travel books. She contributes to a variety of publications, from *Odyssey* to *Alaska Airlines Magazine* and the *Miami Herald*. She has written about golf in Ireland, waterborne safaris in Africa, canoeing in British Columbia, and travel in Vietnam, among other exotic destinations.

When not discovering wineries on the backroads, or enjoying the outdoors with her three daughters and a lively contingent of grandchildren, Karen specializes in golf-travel writing and playing on courses around the world with her partner, Michael Capp.

## GARY CRABBE

Gary Crabbe is the owner of Enlightened Images Photography and the photographer for Voyageur Press' *Our San Francisco* and *The California Coast*. His other clients include the National Geographic Society, the *New York Times, Forbes*, L.L Bean, the Nature Conservancy, and the Carnegie Museum of Natural History. He sells his fine-art prints, murals, stock, and assignment photography traditionally and through his Web site, www.enlightphoto.com.